CONFESSIONS
OF A SUNDAY-SCHOOL
PSYCHIC

LINDA STIRLING

the
publishing
CIRCLE

the
publishing
CIRCLE

admin@ThePublishingCircle.com

or

THE PUBLISHING CIRCLE, LLC
Regarding: Linda Stirling
1603 Capitol Avenue
Suite 310
Cheyenne, Wyoming 82001

CONFESSIONS OF A SUNDAY SCHOOL PSYCHIC /
LINDA STIRLING – SECOND EDITION
ISBN 978-0-9890681-7-8

CONTENTS

DEDICATION

TO THOSE WHO QUEST FOR knowledge and seek to make not only their life better, but the lives of others better as well. As I forever do, I thank Creator and all the abundant soldiers for goodness who help me daily with their guidance.

MY FAMILY IS THE FOUNDATION of my heart:

Keith Sinclair; Randi Hammers Sinclair; Kaden Sinclair; Kari Sinclair; Audra Wanner; Jordan Stirling; Shirley Obermeyer; Frank and Lu Stirling; Sharon Deeds, Donna Nelson; Tommy Neill; Carol Reese; Scott Stirling; Lorrie Stirling; Jason and Janna Stirling; Valerie Mais; Stephan Mais; Misti and Jason Valentino, Olivia Valentino; Brent Giordani; Jacob Giordani; Dillon & Shawntée Dugan; Keira Sinclair; Kole Sinclair; Brooklin Sinclair; Troy Sinclair; Simone Craig-Wanner; Amour & Analise Patterson; Summer Lee Opsal; Adalynne, McKenna, & Cadence Dugan; Michelle Wanner; June Klipera, Bob and Betsy Klipera, Cassie Klipera, Holly Sterling, Bruce Klipera, Travis Klipera, Emma Klipera, Chuck Sterling, Deborah Burnett, Louie Kuebelbeck, Dan Campana; and Joe Campana.

And for
my precious sweetheart,
Steven Campana,
I give thanks
for the sweetness
of our love.

ACKNOWLEDGEMENTS

AS I WALK THROUGH life, there are many who walk by my side. Some have been there for decades and others have more recently joined my journey. All bring richness to my existence.

THANK YOU NOT ONLY for your great love, but for helping bring this book into being with editing support, wisdom, and more:

Cherie Veys; Kate DeVillers; Laura Steward Atchison; Kymm Nelsen; Robert Brown.

Clearly those who helped with the book are amazing friends. I want to recognize these amazing friends as well, for without their ongoing love, support, laughter, and the joy they bring to me, my life and my work would not be the same:

Roy Craig Cook; Alex Laws; Koya Noe; Kiannaa Leighland; Thom Cathcart; Ralph Gardner; Cindy Garreton; Jean Ann Koncos; Carla Voigt; Chuck Arbuckle; Dale Lang; Dave and Lynda Schumacher; Kathy Clements MeGee Weil; Rhetah Kwan & David Kleber; Deb Kloss; Dee Naylor; Gary Porter; Lucy Hammond; Joan Wolf; Judi Jennings; Karylee Harrison; David and Kimmer Goldblatt; Laurie Palmer; Charla Ochse; Mary Vandehey; Nancy Battye; Stephanie Meinhold; Siobhan Wilcox; Susan Davis; Lynda Cook; Michael and Sylvia Eagan; Toni Curry; Josie Phelan; Dannelle Bernards; Vicky Crumpacker; Penny Line; Roger Vinton; Edwina Wasson; Guy Eakin, Wanda Wilder, Sunny Liston, Lorena Angell, Daniel & Maria Fehr; Jane De Forest; Andi and Kevin Crockford; Stephanie Frank; Cliff Edwards; Kimberly Eubanks Soenyun; Mark and Joann Nesser; Mia Bolt; Vickie Helm; and Michele Uplinger.

In all you do,
BE the blessing.

—Linda Stirling

CONFESSIONS
OF A SUNDAY-SCHOOL
PSYCHIC

LINDA STIRLING

**STAY IN THE PATH OF LIGHT
WHEN EXPLORING MYSTERIES.**

CHAPTER 1

As We Begin

'M PREPARED FOR YOU to think I'm weird. Not all that many years ago I would have been looking at my watch and saying I was late for my root canal if anyone had spoken to me about some of the things I'll be sharing with you.

As an ex-Sunday school teacher, instilled within me was the notion that anyone working in the realm of the unknown was unholy. It's odd though—when things start to appear to you, wafting through the air as if they were common as clouds; when you begin to have the ability to see into the future and then that future proves true; when you can influence healing through spiritual means—how your thinking shifts.

A lot of what I'll share with you will be things that may cause you to think, "She's a little off her rocker." That's why

I like to mix in the in the matters that have been verified medically or scientifically.

Not that you still can't think I'm crazy. You can.

The thing is, I used to worry about that, but I don't any more. Seeing entities composed of "thick" energy, viewing the departed and talking with them, experiencing medical miracles . . . things like these are hard to ignore. I had to learn to accept and embrace all that I am and ask that I be guided to serve. My motto is "In all you do, BE the blessing." If the visions I have and the spiritual healing I do don't have that element, then I'm perfectly able to keep quiet and step away. But the parts that are so fun to share, well . . . I hope you'll enjoy what I'm about to disclose. Why do I hope that? Because if you haven't already, I aspire to have you look at life and the great abundance we have available to tap into. If you have already tapped in to the realm of what's beyond current norms, perhaps you'll see what more is possible.

My belief is that this great abundance comes through our Creator and that He (or She, if you prefer) wouldn't make all the wonders visible if they weren't meant to be seen. Our awareness of our connections to each other, to those in other realms, and as a planet is shifting. You get to choose to be—or not be—part of that shift.

My ways of addressing the psychic realm may be a bit irreverent, a bit challenging. Even so, I love sharing to share my journey with you. I welcome you to share your journey, too, for in opening the door to discussion and sharing instead of keeping quiet about our experiences, we plant the seeds for our future, for the interconnectedness we have with all that is.

CHAPTER 2

The First Entities

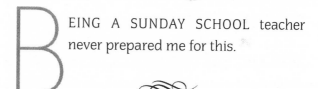

B EING A SUNDAY SCHOOL teacher
never prepared me for this.

THE 64-YEAR-OLD MAN across the table from me weighed
a good 300 pounds. Jim's* shy demeanor and self-effacing
attitude made me want to comfort him. His pallor held grayness
that felt more than skin deep and focusing seemed difficult for
him. I'd worked with him for weeks over the phone and would
make tiny bits of progress, then he'd regress. I'd make more
progress; he'd regress again. The energy work I did would lift
him out of his depression enough that I got glimpses of the
delightful, warm, and intelligent man he kept buried within his
shyness and depression. After each session he'd express how

much better he felt, how he felt enthusiastic about his future. Then, within a day or two, there would be a slipping back to where he'd been when I first met him. Sometimes the slipping back into a dark depression didn't take more than a few hours.

Now, as I looked at him, anxiety and despair hung thick upon his shoulders. A clinical diagnosis had been depression, yet the various drugs the doctors had tried had not succeeded, nor had counseling. After my initial session with him in person, all my work to date had been over the phone. Somewhat reluctantly, I'd suggested I make a house call. I knew the work I needed to do had to be done in person. I hadn't wanted to scare him, but I'd seen entities residing within him.

My reluctance came from the fact I'd never done this type of work before. Was I afraid, I asked myself? Examining the thought, I decided there was fear, though the fear came from the possibility of failing him. As I looked deeper, I realized I'd fallen into the trap of believing the help I could give him came from me instead of the precious energies that flowed through me. Of course, I thought, the human me has limited abilities, so fear is normal. The part of me that connects with the Divine, however . . . that part had nothing to fear. I'd gotten my ministry license just so I could legally do this kind of spirit-healing. I wouldn't back out.

So there I sat, looking at Jim across the dining room table in his home, explaining he had entities within his body which were causing him to feel the way he did, keeping him in a perpetually dark state of mind.

Jim had trusted me so much over the course of our sessions together, yet I didn't know how he'd take this news. He surprised me.

"That's what's going on!" he said. He went on to explain

he'd always felt like the "darkness" came from something outside of him, yet even knowing this he'd felt powerless.

"I'm here because I felt these entities weren't going to go away easily," I said. "I felt I needed to be with you in order to get rid of them."

He urged me to go ahead and do whatever I needed to do.

I stood and began casting these energy-beings out. For twenty minutes or so I worked until I finally felt them release. The moment I felt the entities leave him, Jim let out a big sigh of relief.

"My God," he said," the last time I remember feeling this good I was thirteen. Have they been inside me all this time?"

"It's possible," I said. "I only know they have been there a long time. I'm not seeing when they came in."

I set back down across from him and saw his eyes were filled with tears.

"My God, my God," he kept saying. "I knew something was wrong! I knew it wasn't me."

"I'm just glad I finally saw they were there," I said. "They were doing a great job of hiding." I talked with him for a few more minutes, letting him absorb what he described as "a feeling of lightness." Even his skin tone had changed and I gave a silent prayer of gratitude that I had been given the ability to help this gentle man.

Believing I was finished, I stepped away to use the restroom so I could wash my hands. As I came back into the room, I sat down for a minute to chat. Jim continued to talk animatedly, displaying a side of him I'd never had the pleasure to experience. Both of us were thrilled about what had happened.

Faster than a single beat of a heart, I saw two entities appear. Nearly translucent rushes of energy, one took the form of a larger and more blocky density than the other, with the second entity attached beneath. The closest description I might give would be as if you looked at a thick liquid that could move, this viscosity taking the shape of two connected rectangles, with some of the energy moving forward at an infinitesimally faster pace than the other. The entities bulleted towards Jim's right side, just below his armpit, "anxious" to get back inside his body. They hit with force, the impact moving Jim nearly off his chair. His eyes widened in fear as he realized what had happened.

The state of mind I enter when doing energy work fortunately prevents me from startling and allows me to see things in ways I never would have believed possible most of my life. Because of this—thank goodness—I stayed calm. Even so, another part of my mind reacted in astonishment, for though I had known these entities existed, seeing them in a visible form was a whole other experience. Fortunately, the calm part of me, the part being guided by Creator, stayed focused on the work.

It's okay," I assured Jim. "I didn't do my job well enough. I need to send these guys further up into Light. They have been inside you for a long, long time and you feel like home to them. I'll get them out this time and make sure they are gone for good."

I began all over again, casting the entities out.

This time I made sure they weren't coming back.

WHETHER WE BRING THESE things to us, or even create them, is something I leave open for discussion. I have my suspicions, but what I know for sure is these entities are real and they have an energy that can be seen when one learns how to look for their presence.

They can also get their butts kicked to the curb.

**ROUGHLY A YEAR AFTER THIS PICTURE
WAS TAKEN, I COULD COMMUNICATE
WITH ANIMALS THROUGH MY THOUGHTS.**

CHAPTER 3

Questioning

GRANDMA TOLD ME SNOWBALL had kittens somewhere. At the same time she said I was not to bother Snowball, she needed to be with her kittens or she might not feed them. At only a bit more than three-years-old, the only word I chose to hear was "kittens."

Small enough to tuck myself under the peony bushes that lined the sidewalk, I nestled beneath the leaves so I'd be hidden from Grandma. My quest to get my hands on the kittens began. Knowing Grandma would scold me for defying her, I closed my eyes and concentrated on calling Snowball to me with just my thoughts.

Soon, Snowball sat purring as I ran my hands over her.

"I won't hurt your babies," I whispered. I cast the image of me gently holding the kittens, showing Snowball how her babies would be sitting in my lap. Over and over I stroked Snowball's hair, reassuring her through projected thoughts and encouraging words.

Off she bounded.

I watched as Snowball ran across our large garden, disappeared behind the garage, then reemerged, running towards the root cellar on the riverbank. In a few minutes I saw her start back towards me, a tiny piece of white fluff hanging from her mouth. When she reached me, she dropped the precious kitten in my lap.

Off she went again, returning three more times with kittens that she unceremoniously dropped in the growing pool of white.

"What a good kitty you are!" I told her with delight as I examined her mewing kittens.

Before long, Grandma called. Reluctantly, I answered, realizing when she found me I might be in trouble.

I heard the screen door bang shut and felt Grandma coming towards me. She crouched down beside the peony bush where I'd hidden.

"Where did you find the kittens?" Grandma asked, slightly smiling despite herself. "You know you were supposed to leave them alone." She dabbed at her forehead with her yellow apron. I could smell the dish soap on her hands.

"In my head I told Snowball to bring them," I said.

"What?" said Grandma. Her smile disappeared and her tone snapped the air, making it seem charged with her anger. The softness of her energy had disappeared.

"I showed her in my head that I wouldn't hurt her babies,"

I repeated.

"Leave the kittens alone," said Grandma in a voice she'd never used with me before. She left me sitting there and I heard the screen door slam.

I knew it wasn't the kittens that upset her.

CHAPTER 4

The Gypsy

THE 4-H FAIR IN the tiny nearby town of Cambridge, Idaho provided the chance for those of us who were watched over with a strict eye the rest of the year to experience, however briefly, a taste of freedom. Country kids, me included, waited all year for the fair.

My second year of attendance escalated into a grand graduation: instead of showing chickens, I could now show sheep. A step up, certainly, in my place in the hierarchy of children of farmers. Multiple long barns dotted the landscape. One building existed solely for swine, another for sheep, one for dairy cows, one for beef, and yet another for horses. Then there were extended spaces for poultry, rabbits, and other small animals. Dusty grit swam up wherever I walked on the fairgrounds, but the dust tasted of caramel corn, rotisserie hotdogs, and independence. I roamed the fairgrounds, checking every stall to evaluate the animals and consider my competition as well as relish the animals' perfection. Periodically, I'd head to Main Hall to see if the judges had laid out the ribbons: white, red, blue, and the coveted grand purple, for I also had sewing and cooking projects there, waiting to be judged.

There was pure joy in being on my own, unsupervised, for the first time in my life. I'd even been granted the privilege of staying in the "dorm room", a space nestled under the slanting rusted tin roof of the big Show Barn. Metal-framed cots beneath the sloping eaves spoke to the need of thick sleeping bags for cushions. The dorm room, otherwise a gray metal hothouse, became an enchanted home for dreamy young girls, fifteen or so of us, overseen by two 4-H leaders who were seldom present. Not that any of us stayed there much, for the fair forever beckoned.

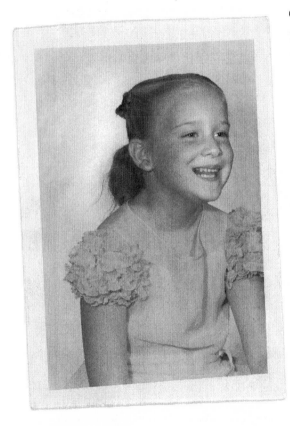

BY THIS AGE, I KNEW TO KEEP QUIET ABOUT WHAT I SAW

With three dollars in my pocket, I sought to soak up all I could. A little carnival nestled its rides between the exercise fields for the horses and the cattle barns. A tame roller coaster, giant swings, a House of Mirrors, droopy Shetland ponies attached to a metal circle-guide, and kiddie rides with brightly colored, flecked metal imagery provided escape from ordinary lives. A few sideshows challenged suntanned boys for their quarters. Farm boys sought to win a gaudy stuffed animal—proof of their manliness—by knocking down wooden milk bottles with a baseball or swinging a mallet that would pop up and ring the bell that announced their strength. When their quarters disappeared, they could toss dimes that would, if they stayed put on the glass surface of upturned dishes, reward them with ashtrays or tumblers of amber and cobalt. For the truly fortunate boys, a goldfish would be won and they could then find a girl to shyly hand it off to, potentially kindling a fair-time romance.

There, too, amongst all the carnival activities—and forbidden to most of my fellow tribe of fairgoers—sat the tent of a gypsy. A sign with a giant eye and the whopping price of $1 written out in bold letters above the message "PALMS" had been affixed to the front. The tent stood slightly apart from the rest of the carnival, almost like an afterthought.

During the day, I hadn't seen anyone enter or exit the gypsy's tent. The dark interior called to me and I ached to see the palm reader inside. Each time I went near, I strained to catch a glimpse of the woman I knew concealed herself inside.

While the carnival had its attractions, most of my time was spent in the sheep barn. I kept the wool of my two Columbians carded and their hoofs spotless, cooing to them that all was okay and that I'd watch over them. My skin smelled of lanolin from repeatedly hugging them close and comforting them so they would feel at ease in this place away from home.

Curfew for those of us who were ensconced in the dorm was nine p.m. The carnival would stay open for another hour, but us 4-H girls would need to be accounted for and ready for our showers and bed while those older than us finished up the night. I had ample time to freshen the bedding for my sheep and fill up their water bucket, so I headed to the barn. A girl screamed in delight as the roller coaster quickly dipped, and as I raised my head to follow the sound, I saw the gypsy. She had come out of the tent to take in the fresh air of dusk. Her eyes met mine.

Across the bare ground she drew me with her eyes and I knew I had to see her. I knew, too, I had stepped into a new place, a place that wasn't evil or doomed. This was merely a different place, a space in the energy of being that wasn't understood well. I'd communicated with my animals before, but communicating with this woman, this gypsy-stranger, gave me a sense of "otherworldness" that I would soon learn would never go away.

I broke eye contact and rushed to finish my chores. Giving my sheep a final hug for the night, I headed to the gypsy's tent. Lifting the canvas flap, I ducked inside and she sat there, waiting for me as I knew she would be.

Brightly colored scarves edged with beading that glistened and seemed to move in the dim light draped every surface inside the tent. A small table held a crystal ball. I knew immediately all the adornments were there as props for an expected setting, that none of the content of that space mattered to this woman. I slid into the chair across from her and did what I assumed was expected, holding my hand out for a reading.

She smiled and I could feel the texture of her thoughts.

She took my hand, though she didn't look at it. Her touch

coursed through me in a powerful pulsing that surged like a river of energy, a tide of connectedness larger than the oceans, bigger than the universe as I knew it. Somehow I instantly accepted that all my experiences were good, that the abilities I had were not something I needed to seek forgiveness for, that they were instead a connection with Divine Source, holy God-energy that I and all humankind had been blessed with, a connection open to all who sought to see. This woman knew the energy of God and she possessed something special in her ability to see through the veils of reality . . . and she saw I could see through these veils, too.

We sat there—me a ten-year-old child with thin pigtails, worn jeans, and a little checkered pink cotton shirt and she, a sixty-something carnival worker—both clearly experiencing an energy bigger than anything we could express.

She seemed to startle, as if awakening from a dream space. She looked down at my hand and began to do the work all who entered came for—a palm reading. I, too, came back from where I'd been and gave a little shudder at the suddenness of coming back to the normal world, wondering if I'd really been in that different space or if I'd just imagined it.

"You will have five children," she said, her energy connection with me now concealed. "There will be sadness, but you are strong." She talked for another few minutes and I fished the dollar bill from my pocket, smoothed it, and set it near the crystal ball. Feeling shy and somewhat embarrassed, I rose and headed out of the tent. That's all I remember of her prophesy, but as I lifted the canvas flap to exit she began to speak and I turned back and looked into her eyes. Our energy connected again, a brief surge, as if to reassure me the connection was real. She said, "You have Knowing."

I KEPT QUIET ABOUT the gypsy.

What I experienced wasn't for sharing with anyone I knew. I recall going back to the dorm, rushing through a cold shower and nestling into my sleeping bag. I remember, too, feeling for the first time that I didn't walk alone. Part of this gypsy's gift was conveying the God-Spirit connection within me and the interconnection of us all in a way that had never presented itself to me before.

Decades later, I laughed as I remembered part of what she'd said—frankly, the part I'd had the most trouble believing: the five children prophesy was fulfilled.

CHAPTER 5

Dancing With Death

MY NEXT BIG EXPERIENCE with the Divine came as I had to choose between living and going into that different realm we call death.

At sixteen, few of us listen. If we do, we hear a jumble of voices inside our heads, and we often choose to override the one small voice that yells, "stop!" I was no exception. After many sessions in the backseat of my boyfriend's car, I was pretty sure I was pregnant. Nowhere among my family or friends was there anyone with whom to share my fears. The only form of pregnancy test was at the doctor's office and going there would mean everyone would soon know my predicament. I'd never thought about the shame I'd feel in this small 1970's town if knowledge of my behavior became public. With reluctance, I realized I had to tell my boyfriend. When I finally worked up the courage, he informed me he wasn't changing his college plans. His message was curt: he didn't intend to marry me.

Despite being brokenhearted over trust lost, I wanted to have this child. At sixteen I thought I could figure out anything and everything, of course, so I didn't have a problem with the idea of having a child as much as I did with the idea of telling my grandmother. The knowledge that Grandma would be upset created a despair inside me that I hadn't experienced since I'd left my mother's house at the age of eight.

The worst I'd imagined became real. Grandma discovered my secret and her disappointment in me reigned every bit as big as I'd imagined. Our relationship had always been loving, her kindness sweet balm to a childhood harboring many troubled days. Now, when she looked at me, her lips drew tight and she wouldn't hold my gaze, as though her disappointment in me tore at her heart.

After spending a day in torment, not knowing how to make things better, feeling I never could make things right again, feeling, too, that I had nowhere to turn, I decided to take my life. Fighting with myself over the instilled belief that to take one's life meant you wouldn't go to heaven, I begged God to forgive me and hoped He would understand how the pain of living felt too great.

Grandma had a large shoebox filled from corner to corner with bottles of pills: pills for high blood pressure, pills for pain, pills for inflammation, for heart problems, and whatever other pills the doctor had loaded on her. Having no idea what might be a lethal combination or how much of any one thing to take, I decided to take every pill from every bottle in the box. After forcing them all down, I went to my bedroom and fell into bed, sobbing over and over with regret for the pain I'd caused. As I waited for the pills to take effect, I gathered small items I loved in order to have them near me and wrote notes that I expected would be read over the next day or so.

The pills did what I'd hoped they'd do. I died.

Inside a place I didn't recall travelling to, I remembered how I'd gone gently to sleep, too numb to cry any longer. This place provided a viewpoint as if I were on the ceiling of my bedroom looking down. Beside my bed, Grandma and her dear friend, Clara, cried as they tried to no avail to wake me. I knew Grandma had read the note I'd left on my bedside table where I'd said goodbye to her and asked for forgiveness for the pain I'd caused.

From my position above the bed, I saw the body I'd inhabited and the still form seemed something of a curiosity. The figure there was me, yet not me.

What was real was the connection to the feeling of my grandmother's sorrow and the knowledge of the pain I'd inflicted. Real, too, was the light around me and above me, a light that blossomed into a tunnel undulating with shades of gold, a tunnel that felt warm, joyful, releasing. The energy of other beings, who consisted of pure love, beckoned. I knew I could go into that light easily and remove myself from the body I'd inhabited. I also knew I had a choice. The pain in my grandmother's heart pulled at my soul.

My love for her drew me back.

With a whoosh of energy bright as the sun, I left the light and my spirit flew back into my body.

My grandmother's joy made coming back a choice I didn't regret, even though times were, to understate in a big way, challenging. Not, however, a challenge because I was pregnant, as it was a false alarm—that time. The challenges, intense and trying, came later. My spirit guides now assure me the challenges were critical for soul growth, as was the lesson of having a choice to live here or in that other world, that other energy-field in time.

I ache for those who, like it used to be for me, have no one to call upon when their despair is as deep as the despair I felt then. I know now that we're supposed to experience this life path until we're called away by a power greater than our own. At the same time, I know Creator's love for us embraces us always. Despite the turmoil that can at times be overpowering in our lives, Creator always operates within the plan set in place, a plan agreed to by us, before we ever took form here on Earth.

KEEPING QUIET ABOUT MY death experience as well as my psychic experiences continued to be my common practice. Tiny feelers were put out now and then, but nothing big happened until, once again, I came close to death.

This dance with death began with a car accident nearly thirty years after I'd met the gypsy.

SITTING IN MY JEEP Wagoneer behind a line of other vehicles as we all waited for the go-ahead from a road construction crew, I sensed danger. Something told me to look in my rearview mirror. As I did, I saw a large white box-van barreling towards me. Time held still as the driver changed from being oblivious to the stopped traffic to entering a state of panic as he realized he'd never stop in time. In that same suspended instant I assessed what I could do, but there wasn't time to move and even if there had been, there was nowhere to go where I wouldn't put someone else at risk. I braced hard on the brake with the hope I could keep my vehicle from plowing into the car ahead of me and injuring that person.

The truck hit. Seven tons of metal crashed against the rear of my vehicle. In slow motion, I felt my brain slide and hit the back of my skull. As it slid, I thought, this is rather like an egg inside a shell. As everything settled back into "normal time", I realized the weight of the Wagoneer had kept me safer than I might otherwise have been. Even so, I was to later learn, I had broken the welds of the metal bars in the seat frame with the force of my back when the big laundry truck hit my vehicle. People got out of their cars and stood, gawking. Other people ran from the sidewalks to see if I was okay, and, somehow, I seemed to be.

Two women, exceptionally kind and concerned, kept insisting I was in shock and needed an ambulance. All I could think of was I had to go get my son from childcare, that if I wasn't there on time I didn't know what they'd do with him. My vehicle, crumpled and with the windows broken out, was still drivable.

With the truck driver's license information in hand, along with the phone numbers and names of witnesses, I went on my way.

Within the hour, the headache of all headaches set in and was to stay for some time and then reoccur with regularity. I'd also injured my neck, my right hip, my right shoulder, and my wrists. The adrenaline that had kept me unaware of the pain dissipated and the struggle to fight the pain became a challenge. That pain, the pain that magnified and never ceased entirely, soon became the center of my life. The constant torment resulted in visit upon visit to doctors of all sorts. The result should have been that I got progressively better over time. Instead, my health grew worse.

Three years later, I was in more pain than when I'd first been in the accident. A new symptom had arisen, too. The end of my tailbone began to feel as if someone had jammed a hot poker up through my spine. Levels of pain increased and never went away. My primary doctor, bless him, did all he could think to do, even sending me to alternative healers, something decidedly outside his comfort zone. Nothing worked.

Along with the known injuries, then my doctor said I had myofascial disease brought on by the accident. Speculations of other possibilities arose, but the bottom line was no one knew what to do to eliminate or, eventually, even lessen the pain. A regimen of anti-inflammatory medicine, nerve dampeners, and a litany of other drugs eased the pain somewhat in the beginning, but as time went on, months of pain turned into years.

Two years after the accident I lived on Tramadol and codeine. A year later I graduated to a cocktail of Tramadol, codeine, and morphine, supplemented with a litany of anti-inflammatory medicines. Pain levels increased to the point where they were never less than a seven and frequently reached a level nine on the pain scale. I worked outside my home, so I would exist on Tramadol all day, pop morphine on the drive home, then lapse into a catatonic state until I had to start all over again the next day. Inside my heart, I knew this wasn't any way to live, yet I didn't know what more to do. Before long, I couldn't walk without the aid of a cane and soon needed the support of a walker to move even a few feet. Finally, I had to bump up the morphine until I was popping pills like candy, the only relief coming when I took enough of a dose to knock myself out.

On top of all the things I was being treated for—although some had no clear diagnosis—a new issue cropped up. I'd gone in for an MRI when my doctor suspected the pain in my lower left leg might be due to a small fracture. The MRI showed something more concerning: abnormal bone marrow. Visits to an oncologist were added to my agenda.

Finally, even the heavy doses of morphine didn't work. I went to my doctor again, hoping for something new that might provide a modicum of relief, but he explained how he'd tried everything he could think of that might help. He shocked me when he said he thought the time had come for me to be on a morphine drip. I mumbled "I'll think about it," and walked in a state of numbness to my car.

I believed my life would soon be over if I went on drip morphine. Wasn't this what they put people on in hospice? Did my doctor really feel there was no hope of recovery? I couldn't imagine putting a drip into my arm and fading out of life.

Arriving home, I knew what I had to do. I didn't want to exist on pain medicine anymore. Somehow, I had to do what doctors had been unable to do. I knew God had the power to heal and I knew, too, that my begging and pleading with God for release from pain—as if I were a supplicant child—hadn't worked. From somewhere deep inside, I knew to get well I had to create a form of partnership, with me as the vehicle who always had a Higher Power inside as well as outside of me. I saw the idea so many of us have of how we heal was different than I'd imagined.

The time had come for me to heal myself.

I collapsed in the recliner that day and began to meditate and pray. For several days I stayed there, off the pain medications entirely, only getting up to use the bathroom or get a drink of water . . . I think, though I operated in a fog. Early on, perhaps in the second day, I began to experience what I now call "lining up", a feeling of energy flowing through me from God or Source, or whatever anyone wants to call this beautiful, love-filled Higher Power. This connection came from both inside and outside of me, a connection to Source energy.

The miraculous happened.

Coming out of that extended meditation, a fullness of love blossomed inside me, unlike anything I'd ever experienced. I knew this Divine energy would forever be within my reach. This expansion of energy gave me the feeling that I had never seen the world before this moment. Awestruck, I saw in all things their magnificence, their intense beauty, their connection to Source, and, dearest of all, my connection to all things and the threads of their connections back to me.

Within a week, I could walk to my car unaided. Within about ten days I could walk around the block. In a few more weeks, I took up dancing, once more enjoying the camaraderie and the dance lessons that had meant so much to me years before.

Now that I had learned to connect with the Divine, I stepped into a realm of the unknown that expanded beyond what I'd experienced in the past. I began to have experiences that amazed me. I knew what the prophets of old had experienced and, more importantly, I knew that as long as I stayed connected to my Higher Power, the power I call God, all that flowed from these experiences would be good and right. Even so, only with reluctance did I begin to share what I was seeing. My reluctance soon didn't matter, for people began to come to me.

They came asking for what I saw for them; they came asking about spiritual healing; and they came asking if I could cast dark energies from them. Oddly, they didn't come because I had promoted what I could do with Spirit's help, for I hadn't advertised these newfound abilities. They had been guided to come for the care they needed. Sometimes they were led to me by friends, sometimes they found me in other ways, but almost always they would tell me they had felt guided. (My belief is that people's guides help them get what they need if they are open to listening to the messages.)

The power of God coursing through me in that time of meditation—and now drawn through me at will—gave me an ability to do what was called in biblical times, work through "gifts of the spirit."

**CHARLATANS ABOUND.
AVOID ANYONE WHO CONTINUALLY
WANTS YOU TO HAVE THEM READ
FOR YOU. TRUST YOUR INTUITION!**

CHAPTER 6

A New Journey

WHAT HAPPENS WHEN YOUR world as you know it comes to a halt? Who do you line up to be? The journey had just begun, and my healing set flame to the tinder of a burning desire to expand beyond my current experiences.

As I harnessed my own spiritual powers, I became aware that we all have these abilities, though many people are taking baby-steps in accessing them, or they mask their powers entirely because they're afraid of what others may think. Some just haven't learned to trust their presence. At the same time, I began to see many frauds who masqueraded as psychics, spiritual healers, and channels, who claimed more abilities than they really possessed. Worse, I saw people who knew how to tap into these abilities, yet used these powers in ways that weren't for the good of those they were supposed to serve. On the other hand, I began to make acquaintance with many sweet women and men who had truly aligned with Creator and other healing spirits. These earth-angels channeled energies and served others with love and kindness.

Once, I'd have been delighted just to find a single person who talked of being psychic, now I ran into them everywhere.

I soon discovered I could see not just the person, but the spirit of other psychics. As expressed, there were some I felt everyone should avoid and there were some I would never allow to put their hands on me simply because they had unresolved issues. As an empath, I didn't want to "absorb" their energy.

These psychics were people who didn't have balance in their lives and sought to use their abilities in ways that put them in control of others. I saw, too, how some energies people are able to harness can be both good and bad. Actually, that's not quite accurate, as energy isn't good or bad, it's what we do with energy. Some people use energy with bad intentions. There wasn't any way I'd knowingly allow someone who channeled energy through a filter that was negative (the filter being that person) anywhere near me.

Seeing through charlatans and evil isn't an ability specific to me, anyone can recognize pureness of spirit. Too often, people brush away negative thoughts instead of trusting their intuition.

I made a vow to never give my power away, and by this I mean decision-making power and an honoring of my intuition—or at least an honoring of it as much as possible, as I sometimes convince myself I'm misreading something. I knew other intuitives I trusted could often give me insight and those gifted enough could do spiritual healing work, but ultimately, I should maintain control.

I learned that although some of us have been blessed to do spiritual healing work, we can't always be successful. There can be factors in the person's body that we're trying to help, or factors in their life journey, that don't allow full healing to take place. Sometimes my best efforts and the best efforts of other healers are not what that person's soul is choosing for them to experience.

Here is where I discovered it could be useful for a person to know what their soul's purpose and their *karma* was about—if they were willing to learn. Many think *karma* is a negative thing and it's not, it's merely what a person has to learn in this lifetime, while the soul's purpose is what we each have to give to others. But more about those thoughts later.

As I tapped into more abilities, it became clear that as a spiritual-healer, doctors were often a critical part of the process for those I served. I accepted that the province of most (though not all) healers is to "see" what is necessary and then direct clients to have their health issue cared for by doctors. Even though I have the ministerial license that allows me to do spiritual healing, I always remind anyone I work with that any spiritual work I do should be followed up with by a visit to a physician—and I make sure they've seen a physician or other medical professional before coming to me, too. In fact, that's a requirement.

Any psychic, healer, or medium who claims to know and see all things is a fraud. We are able to see many things, but we are as children exploring that realm. Just as children do, we have to give our best interpretation of each vision. Sometimes, too, things we foresee happening may not happen for a long time, or freedom of choice enters the picture and the individual takes a path other than the one that was most probable.

Even the best psychics will have their "off" moments when something has intruded to break the Divine connection. Be sure you do your part when this happens and don't demand to receive messages or healing when the person channeling energy isn't at their best.

There are times, too, when the messages we get aren't ones we want to convey. I've been pressed more times than I can count, for example, to see if a relationship was going to work out or if Mr. or Ms. Right was coming soon . . . and sometimes the news is not what the person would like to hear. Would you like to be the bearer of bad news?

The good news is that we all have more control of our destiny than we believe. What we as psychics see is only the most likely circumstance arriving for each person.

Part of the art of living is learning how to create the destiny we desire. A wise psychic will guide you towards discovering ways that help you immerse yourself in that power.

Called upon more and more to do work within the psychic realm, old fears emerged. Then this dream came to me.

I'm in a huge hotel and I can tell there are conferences going on in many of the rooms. Nicely dressed in business attire and in a pair of high heels, I walk down the wide hallway, poking my head inside various meeting rooms as I try to find where I'm supposed to be. Even though I know I'm supposed to be there, an uneasy feeling I'm not welcome bubbles up. I start to enter one room and a guy in a slick black suit yells at me to get out. I hurry along, traveling down the long hallway, determined I'm not leaving, even if someone is rude. Suddenly, a group of three security guards appear.

"Whore!" one of them screams hatefully. "You're not allowed

here!"

"Yes, I am," I say. I feel angry and hurt at the same time. How could anyone mistake me for a hooker? I'm beautifully dressed and look like all the other women here. Then I realize that's just a word the guard is using because he doesn't like who I am. "I have an appointment," I say firmly.

This infuriates the guards. They draw their guns and begin to chase me.

I run, knowing they are wrong about me, yet knowing I need to put distance between them. They intend to do me harm. Sure enough, they begin to shoot.

The desire to get away from them magnifies inside the dream and I run, fear gripping my heart. I feel the energy of fear gaining momentum. Running for my life, I'm able to get far enough ahead of the guards that they can't see me, yet I can hear their pursuit and know it's only a matter of time before they reach me.

A man appears at my side. Dressed in a black tux, he takes my arm. Surprised, I start to pull away.

"I'm here to help," he says.

Sure enough, the guards have caught up and are now right behind me.

"Stand back," yells one of the guards, and I know he wants the man to back away so he can shoot me.

"What do you think you're doing?" says my new accomplice, indignation filling his voice. "She's with me." His tuxedo-clad energy is something to make anyone pause.

The guards back off a bit, but I can feel their uncertainty. They begin talking amongst themselves.

"Move as quickly as you can without making them aware we're trying to leave them behind," whispers the man. He grips my elbow and moves me along.

We get quite a distance away before the guards figure out our sham. Now they pursue us both, shooting to kill.

There's an escalator ahead of us and we run full speed ahead, leaping up the stairs. The guards are out of shape and can't catch us, yet we know they won't give up, that we have to find a way to escape.

At the top of the stairs sets a bank of elevators and we step inside the one with an open door.

A cane appears in the man's hand and I see a knife is imbedded at the end. He uses the cane to lift a panel in the ceiling of the elevator. "Get up there," he says, "they'll be here in a second."

Knowing now that this man is truly here to protect me, I don't question him. I climb into the dark space. I'm only there for seconds before I realize I'm not the only one in this confining darkness. There is a little girl and she's whimpering in fear.

"Come here," I whisper, and I put an arm around the child to comfort her. Her soft little body tucks against mine. I peek through a slit and see a guard has entered the elevator and is questioning my protector. The doors to the elevator close and the guard is inside, only a foot or two below me.

With startling speed, a witch appears out of the darkness of the recesses of the space around me. The little girl recoils in terror and I realize this was what she'd feared. I push her behind me, and though I don't have anything to defend myself with, the witch will have to kill me to get to this child. The witch laughs a nasty, evil laugh and extends her hand, menacing, taunting, as though she knows her efforts to slay me will be of little effort. I see she has needle-thin steel claws for fingernails. She starts towards me, raking the air with her lethal nails. I know I'm dead if she reaches me.

Below me, the man somehow senses my dilemma. Without hesitation, he uses the knife on his cane to quickly kill the guard. With unearthly speed, he is between me and the witch and a battle ensues. The battle is a horrible one, with the man taking many cuts from the witches' talons. I jump in, despite being weaponless, unwilling to let him take all the blows. The witch catches me with one of her claws, and my rescuer pushes me aside and takes her on fully. His clothing is cut and he bleeds from his wounds. An eyeball soon hangs from cords of tissue, yet he casts the witch away.

Now the little girl is gone, too, but somehow I know all she wanted was for someone to show up to protect her.

Inside the dream, the man and I are again walking down the spacious hallway of the hotel, this time in no hurry. "Don't you think someone will stop us?" I ask, thinking his bloody appearance will certainly draw attention.

"Why?" he says. "You have every right to be here."

The feeling I get from him is one of comfort, like I've known him forever, yet he is new to me in this moment.

"Who are you?" I ask.

"Thomas," he says. The sound of his name to my ears is toe-moss. "You spell that with a 'th'," he says, and when I look at him he is all back together again, without any indication of the battle. There's a distinct glint of delight in his blue eyes when he insists upon the correct spelling of his name.

He says his name again for good measure: "Thomas." Then he says, "I'm always here to protect you."

I'd never had a dream of such significance. More important than even the powerful messages imbedding in the dream, I realized I'd met one of my spirit guides. For days, I basked in the comfort of the dream, knowing my path was protected despite those who would challenge me. Sometimes I revisit that dream, taking solace when I'm troubled. Thomas still talks to me, but now his conversations with me are usually outside of dreams. He had a gift for me, too, in his choosing to bear that name. That gift came later.

Through unusual circumstances I met a man with whom I felt a solid connection from the moment we met. I'd had the chance to meet him earlier and had put his invitation to meet off, yet through this fellow's gentle persistence, I finally made time to have tea with him. When we got together, we immediately began to have a great conversation about the spiritual realm and our observations of how people can have more powerful connections with each other and with all of creation when they choose to do so. Within a short time, I realized our friendship was to be life-long. As our first conversation neared an end, I said I wanted to make sure to have his number in my cell phone so I could call him and we could meet again.

He said, "When you write my name down, it's T, h, o, m. Thom with a 'th'. It's short for Thomas." There was a glint in his blue eyes exactly like the glint I'd seen in my spirit-guide's eyes. I'm sure my mouth hung open.

That night at home as I mused over the conversation and all that had taken place in a realm beyond this one in order to have this happen, I realized several things. Spirit-guides can take any name and form they choose; my guide wanted me to know he would always be there, that there is a kind of partnership between this dimension and the spirit world that we can call upon; and he knew the earthly Thomas would be coming my way and that he could manifest his words word-by-word, giving affirmation to his presence.

I realized, too, that the travels within the hotel represented the many times I felt threatened by my beliefs and my psychic abilities, yet I really had nothing to fear. The child who needed protection was, of course, a representation of me.

Thomas, my spirit-guide, and Thom, my friend, are always there when I call on them.

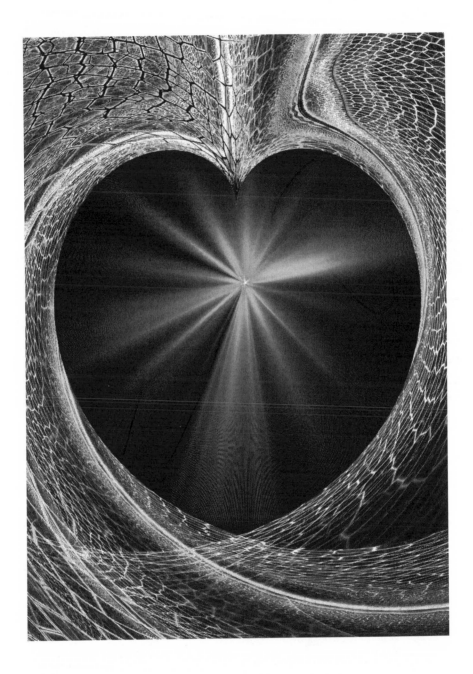

CHAPTER 7

Earth Friends

THE TIME TO STATE publicly that I'm psychic didn't arrive all that long ago—and sometimes I hesitate to even use that word as what I have been able to experience and share is so much bigger. Sometimes I have visions in my head, complete with cartoon-like drawings of what my guides (more about them later) want me to grasp; at other times, I talk directly with spirits who have passed; sometimes what comes in is more a sense of knowing; there are smells, energetic bodies, orbs and other good entities, and more. When I turned the corner of death, a new unchartered world awaited me, a world that resided within my own world and yet apart from this world at the same time.

I'd had no awareness of others who did the same kind of

work. If you'd asked me then who even someone as well known as say, John Holland or Sylvia Browne was, I would have said I'd heard the names, but they would have registered insignificantly within my consciousness. My world had consisted of career-building and raising kids, with little time for other pursuits. I began to read everything I could get my hands on and found many kindred souls within the pages of books. Even so, there was still a reluctance to step out and embrace spirit work as part of my life path.

One of the first "pushes" I had to be public about my psychic work and experiences came when I attended a conference in San Jose, California. There were over 800 attendees. Over the course of four days several people approached me and said things along the lines of, "I had to meet you. I can see you're a healer," or "I can see you're psychic." Naturally these were people who were psychic themselves, yet this wasn't that kind of convention, so their assertiveness and the fact they had been drawn to seek me out and express their thoughts seemed unusual.

Two months later, at a writers' convention, I sat at a table during a lunch break with Alex Laws, someone who's become a close friend through our psychic connection. Alex pairs his psychic abilities with a strong business background. He's a strikingly handsome, clean-cut guy with dark eyes and a flashing smile. I'd invited him as my guest and, with his usual charm, he'd attracted other interesting people.

My focus was directed inward as I mulled over the business book I planned to pitch to an agent in attendance. Alex had said he'd meet me at the casino restaurant and I broke from my reverie to see him waving at me to join him. Two women sat next to him and they were all deep in conversation as I arrived.

Both women were younger than me and had, beyond physical good looks, the kind of intelligence that shines brightly through some people's eyes. After a bit of getting-acquainted time, Alex said to Laura, who sat directly across from me, "You have something wrong with your jaw."

Laura is a petite woman with shoulder-topping, soft waves of auburn hair. Her energy had, from the time I saw her, felt soft and welcoming. As Alex spoke, I looked at him and immediately tapped into his energy and "saw" Laura from his viewpoint, then propelled into a viewing of my own. Without being nudged to share, I blurted out, "I can see you have pain in your jaw, but it doesn't originate there. May I have permission to touch your neck?"

Laura looked a bit surprised, but she smiled sweetly and said that would be fine.

I got up from the table and went to stand behind her. Placing my left hand gently on the crown of her head, I let my right hand be guided by the spirits who work through me. My fingers were drawn to a spot on her lower neck, finding this area to be roughly the size of a quarter and swollen about an eighth of an inch higher than the surrounding skin. I worked on that area and the area of her right shoulder for a few minutes. In that time, I felt the swollen area beneath my fingers become flush with the rest of her skin. As my hands left that spot and I moved around her, I saw the amazement in her eyes. "Wow," she said, "that area has been painful for a long time. The pain is completely gone."

As I sat down, I said to Laura, "There's more there, but I'd like to share that with you in private. Then, if you'd care to, you can share what I tell you with everyone else." She readily agreed.

Before we all left the table to go back to the conference

room, Koya, the other woman with us, began to ask me questions. Koya is a striking, lanky, athletic blonde who has the ability to zero in with targeted questions. I've learned she's a business whiz. She began asking me about some of the conditions she was experiencing in her body and I answered her in ways that validated what she had been told by her doctor.

Laura, eager to hear what else I had seen, suggested we find a quiet nook before we went back to the lectures. She perched on the edge of a brocaded chair, looking at me intently.

I didn't keep her waiting.

"I can't see who this man is, but someone you love died within this past year. He is holding on in the area of your right shoulder and that's why you are having trouble in that area of your neck and shoulder."

Tears sprang up and then Laura began to sob. "That's my father. The spot you touched is where he broke his neck."

"He will always be close to you and be with you, but you have to release him," I said. I hurried to explain as best I could. "There are different realms. Releasing him will let him pass peacefully into the next realm, but that doesn't mean he won't be able to feel you or that you won't be able to feel him. You're holding on to him in a way that won't let him pass."

Laura sensed right away what I was talking about. She dried her tears and thanked me profusely. I saw some other things that were going on with her and asked if she'd mind if I did some energy work to see if I could make a difference. I did some work then, and more later, cementing what was to become a fast friendship.

The next mealtime found Alex, Koya, Laura and I together again. We'd gotten comfortable with each other and this time I was to be the one on the receiving end. "Why are you hiding who you are?" each of them asked me in turn, in various ways.

On the hot seat, I stumbled around, processing what they'd said and trying to explain myself at the same time. My reluctance stemmed from childhood fears of being judged, but more than that, I felt my gifts were from God and that to use them would seem like I was boasting about a power that was His, not mine. They didn't buy any of the excuses I found myself uttering and, hearing myself, I wouldn't have either. Their message was clear: if God gave you these abilities, He meant for you to use them.

Sitting there at that little table with them, they assured me they were there to support me. For the first time, I felt okay about being known publically as a psychic, a healer, a medium, an intuitive, or whatever name fit—no, more than okay—fully willing, supported, and confident I could step into being a psychic and spiritual healer. Looking at their faces, I knew they were part of my earthly team. Although no one else could hear them, I heard a chorus of the unseen singing, "finally!"

These precious friends, and others, too, support me and lift me up when there are challenges. There are, and will continue to be, many challenges, for there are still those in the world who do not believe God can work through ordinary people. They also don't believe in any of the many helping entities who support Creator's work. At best, some of these unbelievers say disparaging things. At worst, they wish me—and others like me—ill.

Here's Laura's story in her own words:

> I had noticed that my health had begun to decrease after my dad died. I had a lot of pain throughout my body, especially in the neck area. My hearing

was decreasing as was my vision and I had bouts of dizziness. Everyone said the vision problem was because I was getting older but it just seemed weird to me because it came on so quickly. I also had night terrors and nightmares pretty much every night and the teeth clenching was beginning to cause dental problems. I also was having a great deal of difficulty losing weight and was craving lots of unusual things for me.

I had this feeling in the back of my head that I seemed to be having symptoms similar to what dad had experienced with his Parkinson's but that quickly got rationalized out of my head as an impossibility. When it persisted, I went to the neurologist who did some brain scans, etc. and said there were no signs of Parkinson's and he was uncertain what was going on. They ran further tests that confirmed hearing issues and gave me some medications for the clenching and nightmares. Nothing worked though.

I was at the chiropractor a few times a week, getting massages regularly and was living on Advil. Then I met Linda.

It was one of those random yet preordained moments at a conference when you know it was God who directed you to meet someone. Linda and I clicked immediately and she commented that she felt there was something going on in my neck and that my jaw was misaligned from clenching. Now, I had not told her anything other than I had been searching for an answer as to what was wrong with me.

As we continued to talk, she pointed right to the area on my neck where the majority of my pain was and she said it had to do with my dad who had recently passed but that he was still here and was attached to me. I realized at that moment that my pain was centered exactly where dad had broken his neck just before he died. I immediately started to cry.

Linda laid her hands on my neck and began to pass a message on to me from my dad that was too detailed and personal to come from anyone but my dad. I could feel his presence, and God's, all around. I felt like I was in a loving yet sad embrace. I had goosebumps and felt incredibly warm. Tears were streaming down my face as I felt Dad begin to disconnect from me and go with God all the way. As he left, the pain in my neck went away and my body felt lighter than it had in a year. I knew that Dad loved me and that we both had not wanted to be separated. With Linda's caring and loving touch, Dad and I were able to move on and tell each other what we had not been able to express when he originally passed on.

THERE'S A QUOTE I like to pass on to those who are so sure they know that what psychics see and hear is false; the truth of it offers, too, a glimpse as to why some healers can do the work we do. The quote is from Neil deGrasse Tyson, an

American astrophysicist and science communicator. He says,

> *"Before you judge others or claim any absolute truth, consider that . . . you can see less than 1% of the electromagnetic spectrum and hear less than 1% of the acoustic spectrum. As you read this, you are traveling at 220 kilometers per second across the galaxy. Ninety percent of the cells in your body carry their own microbial DNA and are not "you". The atoms in your body are 99.9999999999999999% empty space and none of them are the ones you were born with, but they all originated in the belly of a star. Human beings have forty-six chromosomes, two less than the common potato. The existence of the rainbow depends on the conical photoreceptors in your eyes; to animals without cones, the rainbow does not exist. So you don't just look at a rainbow, you create it. This is pretty amazing, especially considering that all the beautiful colors you see represent less than one percent of the electromagnetic spectrum."*

As I've grown into my abilities with acceptance and gratitude, I finally understand how it can be that others don't see/hear/feel the same things I do. All will, eventually, I believe, and more and more people are tapping into these "new" realms on a daily basis. For others, they are finally feeling safe enough to admit to what they've been seeing and hearing all along. I like to think of this as "rainbow eyes to other realms."

CHAPTER 8

Cords Of Love

'D GONE OUT FOR the evening, meeting up with a group of friends. We all danced with different people from our group and laughed at the musicians who wore ridiculous costumes and playfully engaged the audience.

Turning to go back to my table from the dance floor, a man tugged at my arm to keep me dancing. I didn't know him well, but I'd met him, said hello and exchanged names, at a mutual friend's party the week before. The next song was well along when he smiled a bit flirtatiously. Immediately I saw cords of connection floating through space and connecting to a woman hundreds of miles away from where we stood in Vancouver, Washington. The cords undulated and through these undulating ribbons of gold, blue and pink flowed love—love flowing from this man towards the woman I saw in California—and her tentative reach back to him on a corresponding pathway.

Without thinking, I took hold of his arm and pulled him towards me so he could hear above the music. "I think you shouldn't flirt with me when you are bound to Cynthia* in California."

He stopped dancing and took a moment to gather himself, the shock apparent on his face.

"Can we talk somewhere more private?" he asked.

We moved to a corner of the restaurant and he began rapid-fire questioning. From somewhere unknown to me, I not only knew the name of the woman, where she lived, and was able to describe what she looked like, but I could feel the thoughts she had towards him. With all the detail I gave him, he didn't doubt what I was seeing was real.

What I saw showed that a relationship was possible between this man and this woman. It's the paths of possibility like this one that are always before us in all areas of our lives. When we tap into our own spirit-knowledge, we often know—even if we sometimes don't really like the answer—if we will, or should, travel a path or not.

Sometimes we make the decision to travel a path we innately know we should not. Divine Source always gives us this great gift: choice. Just as we have choice, others do, too, so the mix of possibilities widens. When you go to a psychic, it's important to remember that any psychic can only see the most probable path when looking at the future. Although this man had a strong desire to have a relationship with the woman and I could see him pursuing her and her interest stretching out towards him in return, she chose a different path. I'd seen her indecision, but I couldn't see her ultimate decision. Despite her initial attraction, she chose not to have this relationship.

One tough part of being psychic is to know what to disclose or how much to disclose. The other tough part is not being able to see everything the person you're connected to wants you to see for them.

And, sometimes, as I've had to learn, it's wise to keep quiet!

CHAPTER 9

Dreams

AT FIRST, THEY SEEMED like fat rings of a cold gray-metal mass twined around my middle and ring finger on my right hand. Something within me, even inside the dream, wanted to brush them away. As I struggled to get these thick rings off my fingers, they reluctantly released from their circle-shape and became baby coral snakes, one slithering down to bite the pad below my thumb, the other biting the opposite side of my hand.

Within the dream I felt the sharp sting of their bite.

I rushed to assure myself that as baby coral snakes (their colors oddly reversed within the dream-vision) their infancy might preclude serious poisoning. Yet as I dream-watched, the flesh on both areas where they'd bitten me began the process of necrosis, blackening as the venom spread. Absently, I wondered if I would have to cut out the flesh to stop the slow-spreading death. I wondered, too, how my hand would function, should a significant portion need to be removed.

Waking, I had no fear, just as there had been no fear within the dream, even at the sting of the tiny fangs as they pierced my skin. I gave thought to what message the dream might have carried, but otherwise began my morning.

For forty-five minutes or so I checked my email, made some notes of planning, and then I hopped into the shower. After drying my hair, I began to fix it for the day. As I did, I happened to catch sight of my upturned palm . . . and gasped. The areas of my hand that had been black with necrosis in the dream exhibited a vivid purple-black color in those same spots.

I've learned that things that seem unbelievable no longer are. Nevertheless, this was a bit to take in. Not knowing what else to do or what to think of this, I simply went about finishing what I'd started. Every so often, I'd check my hands. Over the course of about half an hour the dark purple-black coloration began to lighten and then, finally, disappear entirely.

What did it all mean? A number of interpretations of the dream have been offered by friends. But as for the reality of my flesh changing color in "real" life, no one stepped forward with an explanation that felt right to me. On my own, I wondered if the twin snakes depicted the intertwined snakes of the staff of caduceus, which many think represents the medical profession, but instead represents commerce and espe-cially printing.[1]

Was this a message to put my experiences into a book? I took this as an affirmation.

I wondered, how had the poison of the snakes manifested in such a way to cause my skin, albeit temporarily, to darken?

Do we live in more than one realm? I've been exploring, experiencing. For me, the answer is "yes."

INSIDE ANOTHER DREAM, I smelled cinnamon.

Cinnamon always delivers memories of my grandmother. Favorite days were those where batches of fresh-from-the-oven cinnamon rolls or apple cobbler sprinkled with cinnamon awaited me when I arrived home from school. Inside this dream, I knew the cinnamon indicated Grandma's presence. Soon she took form and began to speak.

"You have to remember Effie."

"What?" I asked.

In the dream I wanted her to guide me in some fabulous way or spend time talking as we did when she lived in the "real" world. I found myself a bit irritated with her for not following my agenda. Her mission didn't match mine.

"Effie. You have to remember Effie."

Then she was gone and I woke to the lingering scent of cinnamon, a scent that stayed present for several minutes.

While I've never spent a lot of time analyzing my many dreams, the insistence of my grandmother within this dream kept me considering her message. I didn't know an Effie, didn't even know if that was a real name. There certainly wasn't anyone with that name with whom I was acquainted. Perhaps, I thought, this was someone Grandma had known. Even so, why was I supposed to remember her?

My mother had gotten into studying and tracking ancestors, so I decided she might know who Effie was.

"I know you'll think this is odd," I said to her when I called her on the phone, "but I had this dream where Grandma mentioned someone named Effie. Does that mean anything to you?"

What she said next made me smile.

"Effie. Why I'd forgotten her. I have to remember to include Effie in the family history." She went on to explain she'd visited Effie when she was a child. "Let's see," she said, "I think she was married to . . . " she went on to unravel the mystery of the woman she'd forgotten to include.

As for me, I smiled at how Effie used Grandma to convey her message. She hadn't wanted to be left off the roster of names. And my mother had used almost the exact words I'd heard in the dream: "You have to remember Effie."

I'm glad I listened. A dream is sometimes more than a dream.

Our departed, the spirit world, Creator . . . they often make me smile.

CHAPTER 10

Funny Business

This is one of those instances that still has me laughing every time I think of it.

MY DEAR FRIEND KATE had been having considerable pain in her shoulder. She'd had surgery, then physical therapy, and, two years later, should have been fully recovered. Instead, she suffered daily with pain and restricted movement in her shoulder. She had asked that I "look" at her shoulder to see if there was anything she needed to be aware of to allow healing, or see if she needed surgery again.

I'd tried and tried, but for some undecipherable reason, I wasn't getting a message for her. Days went by, then weeks. Still, no message. I began to feel like a psychic failure.

Then, in the middle of a conversation in a coffee shop, I

left my body and had a "visit" with a football field full of Pac-man figures. Yes, wide-mouthed Pac-man figures. At the most distant reach of the field there were many thousands of quiet Pac-men. They hung there in the background, multitudes of back-ups to the more vocal Pac-men closest to me.

Vocal is perhaps an understatement. These guys were screaming.

"We're osteoclasts[2]," they said, their little Pac-men mouths opening and closing in unison. "We're powerful! We can eat bone! We can heal! She just has to believe in us!"

Coming back into my body, I wasn't sure just what had happened, but I knew I wasn't sitting there in the coffee shop a minute longer and trying to have some semblance of a normal conversation. I mumbled my apologies to the woman across from me and said I needed to leave.

Once in the car, I pulled out a notebook and wrote down the word osteoclasts, for this wasn't a term of any familiarity. As happens with these experiences, I knew the message was for Kate and I knew the Pac-men were her cells delivering a message I needed to convey.

Calling her on my cell phone, I began to describe the weird experience and the message from the Pac-man-like cells that had spoken with such intensity. Like all my friends who have experienced my psychic abilities, she had no trouble believing the message was for her.

I drove home. While in the process of looking up the word "osteoclasts", Kate called.

"This is incredible," she said. "I called Dave (a doctor friend of hers) and asked him what he knew about something called osteoclasts. He explained that they're a kind of cell that can eat through bone and smooth the edges where there has been a break. Get this," she said, "he described them as 'powerful'. As soon as you called, I called and left a message for Sarah* and she called me back to say almost exactly the same thing. I guess," she said, "it's time I start believing I can heal." Since Sarah and Dave are both knowledgeable medical experts, I was grateful Kate had their affirmations to give her further faith in her own ability to heal.

As for me, I figure that the great living Universe has to deliver messages in whatever fashion is necessary for my comprehension.

They'd kept this one pretty basic.

WHILE PAC-MAN IS A game and I smile at how the messages come in at times, conveying the messages to others, helping and healing, is never a game to me. I know Creator has a sense of humor and loves our laughter, our joy. At the same time, He seeks to have us work in unison to create wholeness and I take this summons to His work seriously.

One of the challenges I've given myself is to demystify and make practical the abilities I have—for they are far from unique to me. The ability to spiritually heal, the ability to psychically see, is innate within each of us. If we seek truth in all things and are aware if we're trying to delude ourselves and "make" things fit, we are on the right path. I choose to be ready to be who I am, for I can't help others see their callings if I'm not living my own.

God sees our petty quarrels, experiences our turmoil, our doubts and fears, and yet He holds hope that as we all begin to merge in consciousness that we will enter into the Blessed

Space, a space where we see only that which is good and right in each other and embrace each other with love.

I'VE MENTIONED HOW I love to use angel cards. Another tool I use is the Tarot. At first, I'd been nervous about trying to use the Tarot, as it had been my expectation that the cards would be difficult to learn and master. I knew each card had a distinct meaning and that learning all of the meanings was an art. A friend encouraged me to try, saying my psychic abilities might provide me with more information than I thought. At his repeated nudging—and more to shut him up than anything else—I picked up his deck and said I'd try to do a reading for him.

What I saw shocked me.

As I looked at the cards, the back of one card turned a different color than all the others, as if indicating "pick me." I did, and the information came flowing in, a "download" of details of what the card meant and the message to convey. The same thing occurred with the next card, the one after that, and so on. When I was "supposed to quit", the cards quit changing color and I knew I needn't draw any more.

Since that time, Tarot has become one of my favorite tools to use when conveying information and getting answers to questions.

ENTERING MY BOYFRIEND'S APARTMENT, I heard his son Joe's hiccups. Non-stop and loud.

"How long has this been going on?"

"All day," he complained. "I've tried everything to make them stop."

"Mind if I try?"

"No," he hiccupped.

Guides told me where to place just one finger on his head. I touched him there for three seconds.

The hiccups stopped.

Fun stuff, sometimes, what these guides allow me to do.

CHAPTER 11

Other Dimensions

THE WALK AROUND STEIGERWALD National Wildlife Refuge enchants everyone. The birds are one of many treasures there.

One Saturday my boyfriend, Steven, and I had hiked from the highway over to the furthest edge of the park, near the Columbia River. We spent some time enjoying the soft music of the river, the view of snow-capped Mt. Hood, and the cool purple-blue hills that reigned over the scene. The air began to change as the last warmth of the day began to evaporate. The winter dusk would soon be upon us, so we started back to where we'd parked the car.

Intermittently, Canadian geese had flown in. Steven loves them. We would pause to watch their graceful flight each time a small group headed to feeding grounds. In the distance we saw a huge flock gather and swirl. More birds joined them and the size of the flock swelled. We could hear them, even at three or four miles away. I sent up a silent wish that they would gather overhead so we could experience their closeness before we left the trail.

The wish was answered, for they suddenly swung in our direction, flew out in a grand circle, and then flew directly overhead. Thousands upon thousands of magnificent voices rose in such crescendo that everything else seemed obliterated.

Steven pulled his video camera from his pocket and filmed them as the mass of feathered bodies continued to cross the sky non-stop.

Then I heard something more overhead.

A man and two women were talking. One of the women laughed and the group of them carried on their discussion. They were in another realm, oblivious to us, I realized. The conversation went on, and I strained to make out the words.

I looked at Steven, but the sound of the geese prevented conversation.

At last the geese fully disappeared from above as they landed in the nearby meadow.

"Did you hear that?" I asked.

"Yes, aren't they magnificent?" He turned off his video camera. "What a treat."

"Yes, the geese are awesome, but did you hear the people talking above them?"

"Honey," he said, smiling and patting me on the shoulder.

"No, seriously! Couldn't you hear them talking?"

"No. Just the geese."

I knew there was no point asking him to acknowledge something he hadn't heard, so I dropped the subject, frustrated he hadn't had the same experience. He's got what I call "engineer brain" and has to have proof of all he experiences before he considers anything real.

He sensed my disappointment. "Wasn't that an incredible experience?" he said, trying to make amends.

"Yes." I hugged him. "I'll never forget seeing all of them. It's almost as if they created a grand performance just for us."

Later that evening, Steven hooked up the video camera to the computer.

"Maybe we can hear those voices you say were there," he said.

I'd forgotten all about the video.

"Oh my gosh! That's wonderful! Now you'll be able to hear them too!"

He looked at me and I knew he wanted to play the video to prove I was imagining things. With a smile, he began.

I could hear the voices, but only with difficulty.

"Do you hear them?" I asked.

"Sorry, no."

My face must have fallen, for he tried to comfort me then. "Let me try something else. Sometimes the translation from the video camera can be enhanced on the computer."

This was one of those times I was grateful for his great engineer-brain.

He played the video again.

I didn't have to ask him if he heard the voices then. His face said it all.

"Let me see if I can enhance the sound further so we can hear what they're saying."

He tinkered with the sound for some time and we listened over and over. We agreed that the way the sound echoed made it seem the people we could hear were all in a space surrounded by tall buildings. It was clear, too, that there was one man and two women and that they were having a casual outdoor conversation.

About that time my son sauntered in. "What are you guys doing?" he asked.

"Play the video for him," I said, excited to have Jordan hear the voices too.

"Don't say anything," Steven said to me. "Let him tell us what he hears."

Steven played the video.

"Geese flying overhead," Jordan said, looking at us like we were idiots.

"See if you hear anything else," said Steven. "Listen carefully." He played the video again.

"Yeah," said Jordan. "Now that you mention it, I can hear some people. There's a guy and two women talking. It sounds like they're somewhere where there are skyscrapers. Maybe New York City." He looked at us, as if he wondered if we were playing a trick on him. "Why would there be that many geese in New York? Where did you guys get this?"

It's nice, really nice, when there's evidence I'm not completely bonkers.

CHAPTER 12

The Sisters

STEPHANIE, A SLENDER, PRETTY blonde, is an acupuncturist who, through her sweet caring spirit, always seems to imbue a sense of peace to those she treats. Inside the circle of our busy lives, we do our best to make time to see each other every two or three months.

"What are you stuffing down?" I asked, barely giving Stephanie a chance to settle into her chair after we'd exchanged hugs at the coffee shop where we were meeting.

"Nothing," she replied quickly. Too quickly, for I instantly saw her trying to keep from drifting into a conversation about what was bothering her. She blushed a bit, likely realizing she wouldn't get away with this.

"Okay," I said. Then I remained quiet, for I never push, even with friends. I wasn't "seeing" yet, but something big loomed in her silence.

We both laughed at the same time, for I knew then she'd tell me and she knew she would, too.

"This is weird," she said, then laughed again, for she knew there was little that seemed weird to me. "My office doesn't feel right. I've been having problems breathing, too. I think my breathing problems are from what's going on there."

My awareness of her lung congestion hadn't been there until that moment. I realized then, that something big was trying to draw my focus, or I wouldn't have missed the obvious signs of congestion. I mentally shook myself.

"Did you hear," she asked, "about the murder-suicide? It happened near my office." Stephanie went on to say she'd smudged and tried to clear her space, yet the atmosphere still didn't feel good to her.

The incident had been in my awareness, for I had gone to buy grain for my chickens a couple of weeks before and the feed store buzzed with talk about a man who had barricaded himself inside his home earlier that day and set the house on fire. "Didn't you hear?" they had asked, when my eavesdropping became apparent.

When I shared with them that I rarely watch television, they took it upon themselves to be my window to the horror that had taken place. They went on to say when a neighbor saw flames in the house and knocked on the door, the man told him to go away. The man had then fired off a blast from his shotgun for emphasis. As police and firefighters arrived, they, too, were shot at. Everyone was kept at bay. The police and firefighters had been unable to do anything as multiple explosions shook the air. The conclusion was that the man apparently had an arsenal of guns and explosives, so they backed off and called in a SWAT team.

"The police have surrounded the neighborhood. There are still helicopters circling and the schools have just now let the kids go home." Their energy, one of both fascination and fear, had an intensity that clung to me as I went to my car. I said a silent prayer for all involved.

That evening, listening to the radio as I drove to see a friend, I had learned that after a long standoff and perimeter search, the police thought the man had escaped the SWAT team when the house went up in flames. Information filtered through to me from various people and over the next few days I knew residents of the area were wary, believing the man might be hiding out in the neighborhood.

The last news I'd heard was that the man hadn't escaped after all. His body and the body of a woman, whom the police believed to be his wife, had been found in the debris from the fire. It seemed, said the reports, that their deaths were a murder-suicide. Still missing was his wife's twin sister who had been living with them. Presumably, the sister had been away, but no one could reach any of the family to verify where she might have gone. That was the last I'd heard of what had happened.

A chill ran through me as I looked at Stephanie. "That's why we had to meet today," I said.

Stephanie said, "My office hasn't been right since that happened."

I thought of the peaceful space she'd created and the calming energy imbued within that area. "It's clear I'm supposed to go to your office," I told her.

Stephanie's face reflected relief, though she hastened to assure me I didn't have to go.

I appreciated her concern about my time, yet the draw to go to her office became stronger by the moment. No way could I ignore the powerful pull. I didn't bother finishing my tea. I sat my cup down and pulled on my coat. "Let's go."

A half-mile from Stephanie's office, I began to feel the outer perimeter of what in my mind's eye felt like the outside radius of a bomb blast. The energy of the air felt thick, cloying, dark. Then I began to see dark entities bolting about, as if seeking hosts, their black shapes flitting about in the air with an appearance not unlike dark grey kites in an unsteady wind, going first one way, then another, dipping and darting.

Stephanie waited at the door of her office building as I drove up. Her building and a big grocery store across the parking lot swam with ugly entities that stretched out across the commercial area and bled into the residential area beyond. The air here, deeper inside the area I'd seen as a sort of blast zone, had a syrupy thickness that clung to my body like high humidity.

The entities quickly surrounded me, their darkness prodding with an eager hunger. I plowed through them to get to Stephanie.

She ushered me inside her office, and I felt somewhat better here. She said she'd smudged, but the office still didn't feel right to her, nor did it feel quite right to me. She shared that she hadn't been able to work for a few days as she couldn't concentrate and then she had started having the problem with her lungs. I heard her and yet what she said wasn't quite filtering through. I had something much more immediate to attend to . . . there were two women "in" the room. One had partially gone into Light, the other refused to go. Terror kept the second woman's spirit locked in place.

I mumbled something about the energy Stephanie had told me about and said I'd address it later. "There are ghosts here," I told her. "They need help."

Stephanie paled. "What do you need me to do?"

"Stay in your office," I said, indicating the space where she had her computer and did her record-keeping. "They're here in the reception area. I need to talk to them." I explained that the woman who'd died in the fire refused to go into Light until the other woman came with her.

"Her sister died with her, whether anyone knows that or not," I said. "Their energetic bodies fled to your space because you've created a safe haven here. They needed a place of peace and positive energy and yours was the closest they could find. I need to talk to them," I stressed again. "There are entities all around this building," I added, "but I'll deal with them later."

My first priority was to take care of the woman who didn't know she was dead and help ease her into peace.

Because I hadn't heard the full story of what had happened, I asked Stephanie to tell me before I began my work. She shared that investigators had, indeed, discovered the two sisters had both been murdered in the house. Their bones had been intermingled on the bed where they presumably had been placed so they could both be shot at once. Some of the early confusion had been because the bones were so close together, and so destroyed by the intense fire that the police had initial difficulty determining there were two people. The man had killed himself, Stephanie went on to explain, as well as several dogs the couple owned.

Until that moment, there hadn't been any verification for me—other than my own knowing—that this was the woman's sister, her twin, and that they had died at the same time.

Stephanie retreated to her office.

I saw a woman's hand extending down from Light and heard her say, repeatedly, "I won't leave you. I'm not going anywhere without you."

The other woman's terror felt "red" and impenetrable. Her body coiled into itself as she squatted on the floor, arms curled around her knees and head tucked down tight against them. She couldn't hear her sister.

Sitting down nearby, I began to talk to the terrified woman, encouraging her to listen to her sister, letting her know she didn't need to be afraid anymore. Through my mind I projected peace so she would feel a change in atmosphere. Mentally I kept telling her she was safe, that nothing more would ever harm her. "Your sister is waiting for you," I said.

The sister who was partially in Light extended her hand further, urging.

At last, the woman came out of her fear, pushing through the red veil of terror. She lifted her chin off her knees and looked up at her sister.

"It's okay," I repeated, "you're safe now."

Finally, I felt her acceptance. Her fear sloughed off like a garment shed. She reached for her sister's hand and I saw their hands meet.

Their forms melded into a pattern of energy, intricate and golden, laced with other brilliant colors, as they quickly rose into Light together.

The temperature in the room changed as this happened, though I know not why. Perhaps the shift in energy was an acknowledgement of sorts, a signaling of goodbye.

Stephanie stepped into the doorframe of her office, questioning me with her eyes. As someone who is highly sensitive, she'd felt the temperature change as well and it had drawn her.

"They're gone." I shared what I'd seen happen. We were both touched by the profound love the sisters had for each other.

There was more to do. The dark entities that had filtered into Stephanie's space and those who commanded the area around the building couldn't be allowed to stay.

I told Stephanie I would cast out the bad energy in her space, put up shields, and then come back when I had finished teaching that day.

"Linda, are you okay?"

I saw the concern on Stephanie's face and at that moment realized I was struggling to breathe. The problem she'd had with her lungs had manifested in a hurry in my own and caused a sensation that felt like—without a better way to describe it—I had lungs full of molasses.

No wonder I'd been guided to get to this space without hesitation. The combined dark energy of all the entities had enormous power. Even so, I had to put this part of the work aside for the moment.

Assuring Stephanie once more, I went to my car. I could feel my guides and the archangels I always call upon and I gave thanks to them for their precious protection.

As I drove outside the horrid circle of dark energy, I had to pull off the road. My stomach heaved and I emptied its contents. The presence of darkness there covered a broader expanse than anything I'd ever seen. The darkness wanted to consume me and everything else within its path.

I wiped my chin with tissues and found a bottle of water. Yea, though I walk through the valley of the shadow of death, I thought, I shall fear no evil, for Thou art with me. My stubbornness overcame my fear: if Creator needed me to be a vehicle for Him on earth, I wouldn't turn away.

Roughly four hours later I drove back. With even more awareness than before, I could "see" distinct outer edges of the energy blast. This darkness spread out over railroad tracks and into a subdivision in the direction I had driven in from. I paused in the parking lot and took a look around. The dark energy covered an area about an eighth of a mile across. This time I'd been more careful about protecting myself with Light and so when I saw Stephanie she noted my voice was back to normal.

Inside her office the energy shields were holding, but barely. I knew I would have a lot of clearing to do outside the building, even if my only purpose was to keep her space clear—and I wanted to do far more than that: I wanted to send the entities packing.

Once again I went through Stephanie's office and cleansed the air, setting up shields. I went out to the hallway and cleansed that area as well. A door at one end of the hallway lead outside. I had been drawn there earlier when I'd cleansed and had told Stephanie there was another sort of energy there, different and apart from what I'd described to her as blast-energy. I'd told her then that I wasn't sure what this was, but that I'd take care of that situation later. I felt the presence again and simply put up a shield to keep the presence from entering Stephanie's office space.

Finished with the interior space, I told Stephanie I'd be working the outside area for a while and that I'd cover the entire area and cleanse it of any darkness. Before I began, I left her with instructions to call me if she felt any residual energy the next day and that, if I could, I'd drive back to check everything out. My acknowledgement of what had been going on with her lungs, her inability to concentrate, and her general discomfort in her own space helped her to realize how sensitive she was to the energy and she knew she'd recognize it if it returned.

As I began to work the outside area, I could feel the man there who had killed himself and his wife and sister-in-law. He was in enormous soul-pain. I want to stop here and say that when people do horrible things, they often do those things because they have allowed dark entities to enter them (sometimes unknowingly, though sometimes willingly). Dark entities can cloud out rational thought and feed more and more darkness into a person. That person will then often behave in abhorrent ways to others if the dark energy is strong enough. When this happens, a person who might not have otherwise have been a bad person can become bad. That does not mean their soul is bad. Once in a while, there is an actual evil soul, but that wasn't the case here.

I talked to the man and asked him if he was ready to be cleansed in Light. Sobbing and remorseful for all he had done, the day of the murders as well as in the past, he ascended. At another time, I will share how souls go through a progression in what many of us call Heaven, but for now I'll just say he has a learning path, guided by the kindness of Creator and spirit guides, that will eventually lead him back to earth to live out lessons he must experience to elevate himself further in the progression of soul-learning.

The dark entities that remained needed to be cast away. Doing so was the harder part of the work, for they never want to leave a space where there has been pain, fear, depression, anger, murder, or even any negative feeling. They feed upon spaces such as this and want to make their territory bigger. There had not only been the murders and suicide, but people around the area had experienced emotions of anger and hatred towards the man after they'd learned what he'd done, as well as fear before they learned he was dead and they thought he might be hiding in their neighborhood. Dark entities had rushed in to feed. And stayed.

Armed with Creator's Light, I circled the area and cast the dark entities into Light so they could be purified. The process took a long time and I needed to keep my concentration intensely focused on good entities: my guides, the archangels, and other God-loving beings who came to help. When dark entities are doing their best to demand attention, it is easy to break concentration. I knew the great power of the dark ones would capture me in a heartbeat if they could, so as always, I said another prayer of gratitude to God for the help He provides through the many loving entities who always come when called upon.

When I got to the space at the side of the building where I'd felt that "something else," the presence became clear to me. There was another soul there. I "talked" to this soul and discovered this ghost was a man who had been there for a long, long time in our earth years. He'd been stabbed with a knife during a bar fight and died. The incident had taken place just across a fence from Stephanie's office space. The suddenness of the man's death, coupled by the presence of alcohol, had left the man unprepared for what had happened to him and he'd been in that space ever since, confused and wandering, unwilling, or perhaps unable, to realize he was dead. I sent him, too, into Light.

This work is exhausting. I know of some who say, "it's not

me doing the work, so I'm fine." I'd agree that it's not me doing the work, yet for me, the great power of the energies that flow through my human body can be exhausting. For reasons I can't yet understand, some work, such as entity removal, drains me and I need recovery time. Other work, such as healing work, can leave me energized. I love doing both, as I'm grateful to Creator to be used in His service. Even so, it's nap time when I send the "uglies" on their way!

A DAY LATER, I returned to check everything out and make sure all the spaces around and within Stephanie's building felt clear.

One thing that must happen is that when the dark entities are present, you can't allow them to come back or it's much, much harder to get rid of them again. All felt well there. I hadn't intended to see Stephanie, I just checked around her building to satisfy myself, but she saw me and came outside. I let her know all had been cleansed and let her know, too, about the man's spirit who'd been lurking around the back door area. She said that explained the "creepy" feeling she always had when she'd been in that space.

I'm in gratitude that Creator allows me to help in these ways.

It especially touched my heart when I saw the sister grasp her twin sister's hand . . . at last.

THIS HUGE EXPANSE OF dark energies had come in because of what had happened there. Murder, carnage and fear attract these dark ones more than anything else. We each have to guard ourselves, for it's not only those horrible situations that can attract entities. Deep depression, hatred, and other negative feelings within us can attract them as well. So can the energy of anger or being a person who doesn't forgive others. That's why keeping a positive outlook, being forgiving, and searching for what's right in the world is important. We all have the power to call on our Higher Power, by whatever name we use, to protect us from evil.

CHAPTER 13

Light Against The Dark

MURDER AND OTHER DARK situations can draw in dark entities. So, too, can people. Unfortunately, there are those who call to evil willingly, purposefully bringing it into a place with the intention of using evil entities to do harm. Ultimately, evil consumes the soul of those who call in this energy, but those who choose to call in evil either don't believe that will happen when they draw in dark entities, or they convince themselves they can somehow become stronger than the dark forces, or even that they have the power to control how much of these forces they allow in. That is foolish at best. Soul-eating at worst.

I GOT A CALL from my friend Roy Craig. He owns a rental that has one bottom unit and one upper unit. He had mentioned in some previous conversations that he was having problems with the woman who rented the upstairs apartment and he was trying to evict her for nonpayment of rent. He'd said he got "bad vibes" from her, but I hadn't paid a lot of attention. This phone call made me listen.

"I'm starting to get scared," said Roy Craig. "This gal's sister came by and I talked with her for a bit about what's going on. She shared with me that her sister practices black magic, devil-worship kind of stuff. Can you see if that's what's going on? I'm scared to deal with her."

I "went in" and as I did, I felt a huge evil presence travel back to me upon the inquiring thread I had sent. I severed the contact as quickly as I could. This, the darkest entity I'd encountered, had immediately felt my presence and rushed towards me, aggressive and hungry, wanting to consume my light. My body shook, for I hadn't protected myself as well as I should have for this unexpectedly large evil.

When I called Roy Craig back, I told him to be extra careful, to avoid contact with the woman if possible. "Go through the courts to evict her, but don't confront her yourself." I shared with him that I'd seen a horrid dark being there.

"What can I do to protect myself? And what about Rob?" Rob was the tenant in the downstairs apartment and a deeply spiritual man.

"I'll go in and put up a layer of protection all around Rob's space. Have him put rock salt around his door frames and windows, and crystals if he has them. As soon as she's out of there, I'll come clear the space."

The woman moved out of the apartment within a few days.

Tied up with other things, I couldn't get to the apartment right away. Roy Craig called in a pair of light-workers to clear the space. He gave me a report.

"They used crystals and they smudged. I was there when a lamp flew across the room at the guy. The place feels better than it did, but it still doesn't feel right to me."

I promised to make a trip there the next day.

Walking onto the property, I felt a vortex. The open mouth of the vortex stretched almost to the street, and made a rough circle that took in one part of an adjacent home. Vortexes are not good or bad, they are merely, as I see them, a conduit. I suspect they are used as a mode of travel, both for extraterrestrials, entities, and for life forms here on earth with which many are not acquainted. I also believe there is some element within them that allows for an enhancing of power, if the user knows how to take advantage of such. Vortexes are scientifically verified as having a different gravity than other places. Many are well known and some have even become tourist attractions. Old maps will often show vortexes.

The presence of the vortex made the whole situation different. I knew I had to be exceedingly careful.

Roy Craig unlocked the apartment and I could feel the presence immediately. The dark heaviness lunged at me as a panther would. I'd surrounded myself with Creator's Light and had asked the archangels and my guides to walk with me, so the entity's efforts didn't frighten me as he'd intended.

Calmly, I went about my cleansing work, travelling up the stairs to enter the living room. As I did, the entity pushed me from behind, causing me to stumble. The power of this one was enormous, yet I kept at my work. I knew fear would allow the entity to consume me. I couldn't even consider backing off from this dark one.

As I finished my work in the living room, I entered the bedroom. Immediately I knew this was where the woman had cast spells to bring this entity to her. Roy Craig later verified that's where he'd found some of the materials she'd used.

The entity ran its energy up the back of my head, ruffling my hair, showing me how it could manifest the physical. Taunting, it tried to frighten me out of my Light connection long enough to pounce. I stubbornly kept going, clearing, cleansing, and bringing in Light to every surface, every molecule of air.

At last the dark one was gone.

CHAPTER 14

Demons

The next dark entity I had to deal with
was the darkest of all.

WHILE ON VACATION, I got a call. The woman got my voice mail and she quickly explained a friend had given her my number. She said she wouldn't have called, but she felt desperate. Would I please call her back?

Ordinarily I wouldn't have done so. Most things can wait. This one, my guides told me, could not be put off. Even though it was late when I finally had a moment to call, I called her back.

When I got her on the phone, her desperation became even more apparent. As she began to talk, I felt the demon searching for me. Having surrounded myself with Light before I'd made the call, I left him frustrated.

I assured the woman, Rose*, that I'd clear my calendar and

see her the day I returned.

THE FRIEND WHO'D REFERRED her had shared with me that every time he saw Rose she'd lost more weight. She couldn't have lost much more, for at about 5'6" she must have weighed little more than a hundred pounds. She expressed gratitude for my willingness to see her.

"He's been poisoning my food, getting in my medicines," said Rose. She'd already shared that she felt a demon was after her, that, at times, he even inhabited her body. "He's especially bad in the middle of the night. He throws things and does evil things to frighten me."

Rose tucked her chin down, almost shyly, as if telling me all this was almost more than she could manage. Then, as she raised her head up to look at me, the demon appeared, taunting me through Rose's eyes. Her face transformed, altering the size of her head and even its shape.

As I looked into her eyes, they took on a size and cast unlike her own. The demon's face, much larger and broader than Rose's, had a square shape and his skin possessed the hue of red mud. Orange-red eyes flickered with depths of hatred and promised consumption. He grinned. The horrifying grin was full of evil challenge. He held my attention with that challenge for a few seconds, then disappeared and Rose's face re-shaped itself in front of my eyes.

I know this image is redolent of cartoon images of demons, yet that is exactly what it looked like. I didn't pause to think of this at the moment—I had work to do.

I took Rose into the room where I planned to work on her

and sat her down. I explained to her how she would feel the departure when the entity left her body. (I didn't want to frighten her with the explanation that this really was a demon, though I'm not sure why as she knew exactly what this presence was.)

I circled around her, talking quietly. I told her I'd send the entity into Light, so he wouldn't attach to anyone else. The demon glared out at me once more, hatred spilling from his fiery eyes. Keeping at my work, I continued to call in angels, beings of Light, and forces from God to help cast the demon out. I asked Archangel Michael to surround me so I could feel his comforting presence. Then, in half a heartbeat, the demon fled.

As he did, I felt Rose's body lighten in a way that shows me a change has taken place and that a person's connection to their own spirit is unhindered. She'd felt the demon leave, for she looked up at me, the awareness bringing a soft joy to her face. She stood, then fell against me, sobbing like a child.

"Thank you. Thank you."

I held her in my arms. "You're so welcome. You've been so strong. I know how hard it must have been for you. Most people wouldn't have believed you." She cried some more and I held her, patting her back, waiting for her to gather herself. "It's okay now," I reassured, "he's really gone. He won't come back."

"He was everywhere," she said. "I couldn't keep him out of anything and he tortured me day and night."

"No more. You're fine now and he's gone forever. I want to work on your head for a bit, because when these things happen they create a residual energy that needs to be eliminated. May I have permission to touch your head?"

Rose nodded her agreement.

One of the things I often find is that, for a whole variety of reasons, most unrelated to entities, the skull has indentations or bumps on it that my fingers are guided to in order to change a pattern, assist in healing, or eliminate negative thinking.

Rose's skull had a deep crescent-shaped indent on the left side, a bit of a trench really, about three inches long. On the right side, there was a circular lump of about an inch in circumference and 1/4" of height. With guides working through me, I ran my fingers over those areas until the bone lay smooth. I talked some more to Rose, explaining how when people get engaged in a pattern of fear, or any other pattern, their brain becomes accustomed to the messages it receives and creates a kind of groove, not unlike the grooves that were on old vinyl records.

I told her the brain can keep that groove even after the reason for fear has disappeared. Then, having learned to always double-check, I went back to her skull to see if the smoothing had "set." The misshapen areas had returned, but not to the same amount of definition. I worked upon them once more, making sure they stayed even.

As we finished, Rose, stood and hugged me again. "You've no idea how grateful I am." She turned to pick up her backpack.

I noticed for the first time that every zipper had been fitted with a tiny lock. She'd been doing what she thought might work to keep the demon out of her things.

My heart reached out to her once more.

CHAPTER15

Protection

A LESSON EARLY-ON WAS that I need to draw protection around me when I work. Having never studied with anyone, I learned the hard way that my health could be at risk if I didn't call in the light of Creator, my guides, archangels or other helping spirits.

Dark energies have a sort of "residue" that can make anyone ill, and I'm no exception. It took a few times of having my lungs fill with fluid and other highly uncomfortable physical sensations for me to realize I hadn't protected myself well enough before embarking on my work. Now I make sure, especially when casting out an entity or demon, to surround myself with holy Light and call on those who serve Creator to shield me. I make it a practice as I say my morning and evening prayers to ask for cleansing and protection. There's a little ritual

I go through several times each day to draw protection around me. If you'd like to see my ritual, send me an email at admin@ yourlovingspirit.com and I'll send you a copy.

Apart from the physical ailments dark entities can bring, anyone who is an empath can take on the pain of others. That is a core way for some of us who are medical intuitives to know what is wrong in the bodies of others. Sometimes I just "see" what is going on, other times I feel it . . . and feel it deeply.

MY FRIEND DEB* HAD a granddaughter whose health had been failing for over a month. Most of that time, Susie* had been in the hospital. I'd connected with Susie the year before. Her life had been destined to be short and I knew when I'd first seen her she was an angel sent to help others with their lessons.

Having been provided with the knowledge upon the child's birth that she wouldn't live long didn't do anything to diminish the pain Deb felt as she rocked and soothed Susie at the hospital and awaited the inevitable. I'd connected with Deb multiple times a day over the weeks that Susie had been hospitalized. Deb rarely left Susie's bedside and the strain of Susie's hospitalization fell heavy upon her shoulders.

Deb had little support outside of one or two close friends. She would frequently call me when the nurses sent her out of the room so they could adjust equipment and take down data for the doctor. On these few times away from Susie's side, Deb would brush aside my concern over her and ask me what Susie was feeling, for the little girl had never been able to speak. I could "go in" and see what was happening and I reported whatever felt right to share with my friend.

The time for Susie's passing grew closer.

One afternoon as I was working, I felt Susie inside my body and knew as soon as she passed from this realm. I quickly texted a message to Deb, doing what I could to comfort her.

Susie's lungs had finally filled up, despite medical efforts to keep them clear.

Over the last week of "going in" to check on Susie, I had slowly developed pneumonia, my own lungs taking on the sensations Susie was experiencing.

Despite the precautions I try to take, sometimes there are instances where my caring supersedes my caution and I rush in to help. I've had to learn that these situations where love and caring are the guiding energy are just as able to bring physical harm to me as are the dark situations.

As is said frequently, "it's all energy."

IN THE MIDDLE of the night I woke with intense knee pain. Never having had knee pain before, I sent out threads of inquiry to find the pain's origination.

The next morning I called my good friend, Kate.

"Did you have knee pain last night?" I asked.

"Yes. My knee hurt horribly," she said. "It still hurts. How did you know?" She caught herself. "Of course," she laughed.

"Try to keep your pain to yourself," I told her. We both laughed some more as I shared how I'd abruptly awakened, feeling the agony in her knee.

While we laughed about how, through our close friendship, I had connected so acutely to her pain, it really wasn't a laughing matter. My desire is to stay healthy, never to go back to that place of despair when I was so ill. Health means, among other things, I can serve in the ways I am destined. Again, it is prayer and consistent Creator-connections that provide needed protection for me. I try to remember that when I'm so exhausted that I want nothing more than to close my eyes. No matter how tired, prayer is on my lips before I sleep.

I've heard other psychics talk of how they are never worn out or tired by doing the work that they do. A few have offered in preachy tones that "the energy flows through them" so they aren't affected. Good for them, I say. I know the energy flows through me, too, but it's the human me that has the experience. I will say that the type of work I do affects how I feel afterwards. I've mentioned this before. If, for example, I'm channeling healing energy, I sometimes have a sense of euphoria for a short time afterwards. After casting out demons, on the other hand, I can be exhausted for days.

All humans see and experience things through our own lens. It's good for each of us to remember that our perceptions are colored by our experiences—and everyone's experiences are different. Before we judge anyone or rush to conclusions, we should keep this in mind. If we all practiced this, we'd have a more loving world.

CHAPTER 16

Holy Energies
And
Dark Energies

'VE USED NAMES FOR unseen beings throughout this book and I want to expand on what those mean to me and my experiences with them. Giving a name to each energy is challenging and no description can fully depict each of the multitudes of entities that surround us. I'm categorizing with some broad brush strokes, though as you begin to experience more of the psychic world around us, you'll begin (if you haven't already) to have greater clarity than I can provide here. With all that disclaimer aside, I provide definitions as I see them. Along with my descriptions, I want to share with you more of the experiences I've had with them.

God or Creator (or whatever name you use) connects with holy entities to aid them in their key mission, which is to help and guide. Other entities often try to lure in spiritual neophytes by masquerading as being good, perhaps even doing something good at first so that you will trust them. As soon as you do, you have opened a path for them and they will then slowly take over. To be sure I'm connecting with holy energies, I always say "only those who honor goodness and the Divine Creator can assist or have voice." Placing a God-connection as the mandate for allowing their presence always works. If you work with entities at all, absolutely do not skip this step.

Recently, a young woman who believed she could cast out entities came into my awareness. I saw right away that her ego was in control, that she loved the limelight. She didn't realize what enormous powers the dark forces have, or I don't think she would have been so cavalier. Handling these energies is not some magic trick or game. If you're fortunate, you'll escape with some lesser damages, but you truly risk not only your life, but your soul, when you engage with dark energies. If you want to learn how to do this work, ideally you'll learn with a master teacher.

Proceed with great caution. Always, always, ground yourself and call in protective entities (assuming you know how to tell the difference!) to surround you when doing any type of energy work, especially when working with entities and, perhaps needless to say, but I'll say it anyway, with demons.

I've been around other spiritual healers and energy workers who have said, "Don't speak of dark forces, or you draw them to you." While I respect their opinions, it's my belief that if you pretend darkness and evil don't exist, it's the same as saying you're willing to allow negative, even black, energy to be around. I believe it's critical to shine a light on darkness of any form and do all that can be done to eradicate it from the earth.

The Law of Attraction would reason that if you think about darkness you draw it to you. What I see is that sometimes people need a little boost. An analogy might be that you shouldn't give a starving person a feast. If you set a huge meal before someone who is starving, they will get sick when, in their extreme hunger, they eat everything set before them. If you give them a bit of food, enough to settle the hunger pains, after a while they will be able to eat a bit more and manage to eat on their own. I see helping people who are possessed by dark entities in a bit of the same way. It's just giving a hand so they can become strong enough to manage on their own. When a person is full of despair and darkness, just a little light can make a huge difference and help them move into a better space, then a bit better space than that one, and a bit more than that. Now that's in line with Law of Attraction!

So when you're helping others, you want to always call on those who are always in the Light. That's what I call the holy energies.

The holy energies include most angels (don't forget, the devil is said to have been a fallen angel, so you still need to use God as your control here; don't call in angels without setting up the criteria that they are from God when you do); the archangels; uncountable guides; workers in the Akashic Records (more about this later); loved ones who have passed; connected souls who are in higher realms; many whom we call aliens; and many of those we take for granted, such as most plants and our beloved animals. There are many, many holy energies. Some of the holy energies have enormous power and others have more limited powers, but all have the shared element of goodness. We would do well to remember that even in the darkest moments the holy energies far outnumber those who harm us or wish to do us harm.

The question many pose is "If there are so many good entities, why do horrible things happen?" In my work with guides and going into the Akashic Records to learn, I have gotten these messages:

Soul Mandate Number One

Our souls make agreements before we come to earth to have certain experiences. The experiences are designed to do two things. The first is to give us choice. Choices either move our souls further up in our soul-growth, or take us back to do further learning through the process of reincarnation and thereby give us another chance to learn a given lesson. We all go through the reincarnation process to learn one or more key lesson each lifetime. Through the agreement our souls make, we have the experiences that will enlighten us—whether or not our choices are good ones. As Sylvia Browne said in book two of *Soul's Perfection* "Through the heartaches and trials of life, people gain knowledge."

Many of the experiences we choose as souls are not anything we would ask for in our incarnation on this plane—things like rape, or disfigurement, abusive relationships, and so on. How we handle these things is a test for our soul. If, for example, there was a rape, do we go out and harm others because of this or do we use our pain to serve others?

You have heard stories of those who raped and killed and you later learn they had abusive, horrible childhoods. You have heard stories as well about those who had nearly identical backgrounds, yet they went on to use their pain as fuel to start missions to help others. It is difficult for us to say that we "ask" for any horrible experience, and I rush to say we do not do so *in our current consciousness*. That is why we must keep at the forefront of our mind that we are all here to learn and grow and be of service to each other so that when we eventually obtain a greater awareness of our connectedness we will be able, at last, to extinguish any kind of pain.

Soul Mandate Number Two

This is a harder one to swallow for many of us: we also chose to bring each other learning, and sometimes that learning is from ugly things we do (even things that seem inadvertent on this plane) or things that others do to us.

In the realm most of us call Heaven, we work with many wise ones, our spiritual guides, to figure out the lessons we need to learn in each of our incarnations. Other souls who will incarnate with us join in the discussions to see how they can aid us in learning those lessons. Sometimes we are the instruments for learning for those souls and in other lifetimes those souls serve us by giving us opportunities to learn and elevate our spiritual growth.

As creators, we are always trying to move forward, expanding our awareness, our learning, our abilities to create even more. Some creating and learning is exploratory and fun. Other creating is the creating of character development. Unfortunately, or so it would sometimes seem, character development can come at a cost that many think is too steep. It's the wise man or woman who realizes that each experience moves us forwards or backwards in our spiritual growth.

If you watch a toddler as they begin to walk, you see that they have lots of starts and stops, falling on their rump more often than not. Eventually, they learn that if they put one foot in front of another and reach for an object such as a chair or couch, they can reach that goal. After some time of taking these testing steps, they learn to walk on their own. Just as a toddler must try and fail, then try again in order to succeed, we have a similar progression with our spiritual growth.

If you are prejudiced in this lifetime, for example, you may be the victim of prejudice in the next lifetime so you can see how that feels. In the lifetime after that, you will have a choice point to be prejudiced or not and how you make that choice will either move you forward or backward on your climb to spiritual enlightenment.

In any lifetime there may be several things we're here to learn that have the possibility to contribute to our evolution. We may conquer some of those challenges, just as the toddler reaches the couch, and we may fall on our figurative backside with other challenges. So goes the evolution.

We can only do our best to stay upright on as many fronts as possible.

CHAPTER 17

Angels And Archangels

NGELS AND ARCHANGELS ARE happy to be called upon anytime. They can all serve us, though some have greater abilities in specific areas. Even those with less specialized abilities have abilities far exceeding our own. Doreen Virtue is one of the individuals who has written and spoken at length about calling upon these heavenly forces. I'd encourage you to connect with some of her writing to explore how you can connect with angels and archangels.

There are some angels and archangels that I have a great affinity with and so I call on them more often than others. Like many lightworkers, I commune with Archangel Michael and call on him when I need the resources to overpower great darkness. I also adore Indriel, Akasha, and Archangel Gabriel. While angels and archangels all have many specialties, perhaps developed because they were called upon by God to serve in specific ways, any angel will come when you call upon them.

It's important for us to remember that none of these heavenly workers can override free will. They are here to assist, not take over our responsibilities and, most importantly, they are here as messengers—when we choose to listen.

MOST PSYCHICS HAVE TOOLS they use, and I'm no exception. I also love to use them as much for myself as for others. Perhaps the tool I love the most is my set of angel cards.

I'd been feeling a bit down and despite using all my energy to "line up", I couldn't shake the negativity. Knowing I had a multitude of ways to lift myself up out of my funk, I chose first to draw upon my angel cards. Among the draw was Archangel Michael. A few days later, I had another issue to solve. Archangel Michael showed up again. The pattern had just begun. Whenever I had a personal issue to consider or I needed an emotional boost, Archangel Michael showed up.

After a few weeks of this, I became convinced I'd somehow come to visually recognize this card. I thought, there is a fix for that! I closed my eyes when I drew the cards: he showed up again and again.

What love these angels have for us!

If you want your own angel cards, the ones I use and love most are *Messages From Your Angels* by Doreen Virtue. There's a link on my site, **www.YourLovingSpirit.com** if you have trouble finding them.

CHAPTER 18

Guides

'VE DISCOVERED MY GUIDES through various ways, though the two ways that stand out are through dreams, as I shared in the previous section about dreams, and through hypnosis. One thing I see happen is that people try too hard to "make" their guides become apparent to them. This isn't something that happens with forcing. Instead it's when one relaxes and allows the guide to come into awareness that a person is most successful in connecting. If you want to learn more about ways you can connect with your own guides, I share more about this on my website.

Everyone has guides. When we learn to connect with our guides, they can help us in sometimes unfathomable ways. For many, guides feel like a small voice in one's head that can be differentiated from inner dialog. Guides can be people who've passed on and want to help us with the knowledge they now have. Guides can also be entities from other worlds.

Guides do just that: *guide.* They aren't decision-makers and they can't intervene in the way that angels sometimes can. Even so, they are extremely valuable to us. They can help with decision-making by providing additional information, guide one's hands for healing—often using their skills from a heavenly realm, skills we don't currently possess—and they can alert us to danger, and so much more.

My own guides are primarily three individuals who have lived in other times. I swear ninety percent of the people in the U.S. who say they have guides claim to have a Native American guide. I've not taken the time to find out if there really is a proliferation of Native guides, or if people merely like the idea. With that all aside, one of my guides is Native American, and he tends to not say a lot unless asked or if he thinks there's danger. He's got protector-energy to him, as do each of my three primary guides.

I first met Vaive Atoish in a past-life regression. He wasn't part of that time I travelled back to, but I saw him there and he let me know, telepathically, his purpose was to watch over me. When I saw Vaive Atoish in that regression, I sensed, as he looked at me, that he didn't belong there, that he'd simply wanted to connect. Immediately, I felt the bond between us and I intuited then that he'd never leave me in my current incarnation.

Since my first awareness of him, he has come to me in dreams many times. When he speaks to me at other times, I don't see an image of him, yet I know who he is from the energetic marker he projects. He is—and I use the present tense, for he is very much alive in this realm—wise and deeply caring. For some reason unknown to me, Vaive Atoish has not let me regress to the time I was with him in another life, yet I know we were connected.

While Vaive Atoish and I were connected in the past, that is not the case with my other two primary guides.

Thomas' first visit to me was inside that night-horror dream where I ran, terrified, and then met up with a dark, evil being. Thomas came to me, as I shared before, and let me know I was protected. I'll never forget the intensity of his message and the comfort he gave me. "You are never alone," he said. "I'm here to watch over you."

When I came out of the fear that I'd felt so strongly in that dream, he sat with me and I absorbed his calmness, his essence of quietness and peace. Thomas is a rather ordinary white man, his features rounded and soft, and there is a tonsure of pale white hair circling his head. His blue eyes twinkle, though not with mischievousness, more with the feeling that he finds joy in all things.

While Vaive Atoish is all seriousness, Thomas has never shown himself to me without a smile. He wears a light-colored robe of coarse texture and there are crude sandals upon his feet. I feel the consistent presence of Thomas.

Akeela is a fire-spirit. I mean that in the sense that she has intense male energy for a woman. She came right at me in the middle of the day, no waltzing gently in through dreams to introduce herself. I laugh at her sometimes, for she is forceful and reluctant to guide, wanting more to tell me what is in my best interest. It's funny when I feel her holding back. She feels kind of like a big sister who is impatient that I'm not "getting" things as quickly as she thinks I should.

Akeela has skin that's dark as midnight with a beautiful

blue polish. Her hair is short and she fills it with, it seems, anything she fancies. She often adorns her body with an assortment of beads and feathers, and she has piercings that she emphasizes with bands of hammered metal.

Sometimes she wears no adornment at all, looking as if she's just oiled her skin. I adore her and sometimes feel as if I'm the one who's doing the guiding, calming her down. Just when I think I'm the one offering guidance though, she'll surprise me, coming in with wisdom and strength when I most need her.

Each of us have many, many guides, though some are more connected to us than others. Some guides will only have a presence when called upon or when they see you're in need of their help. Just as John of God has guides who work through him so he can do healing work, I have guides who help me with medical intuition. Other guides are with me when I call on them for different purposes. Sometimes my guides pop in when I least expect them! I hold them in great reverence and make sure to thank them for their help.

CHAPTER 19

Aliens

PERHAPS THERE ARE THOSE who use aliens to help them with their daily lives, but I'm not currently one of them—though they may be helping me without my knowledge. Aliens surround us and live among us.

My favorite "other" beings are orbs . . . at least at the moment.

Roy Craig, the dear friend I've mentioned, asked me if I'd ever seen orbs. When I said I hadn't, he told me there were photographers who were taking pictures of them, that orbs couldn't be seen with the naked eye, yet they seemed to be everywhere.

Curious, I picked up one of the books he'd mentioned and read about the work of a few people who felt they had discovered a new earthly presence of which most people weren't aware.

If you're interested, the books I've read are *Orbs, Their Mission & Messages of Hope,* by Klaus and Gundi Heinemann or *Orbs, the Veil is Lifting,* a DVD by the same authors. I like this information immensely because Klaus contributed a scientific perspective. He holds a Ph.D. in experimental physics. He worked for many years in materials science research at NASA, UCLA, and as a research professor at Stanford University. The one area where I found my beliefs to differ from what was shared in the Heinemann's book was in their belief that orbs have faces. I do agree that orbs can take on the appearance of having a face, however I think it's our nature to try to find some way to make all things relate to us in some way. Putting a face on an energy being is, from my perspective, one of those ways. While many energy beings do have faces, of the many thousands I've now seen, none have had faces.

Another favorite book about orbs, partly because of the pictures and partly because of the enthusiasm that comes through the author's writing, is *The Incredible Light Beings of the Cosmos,* by Antonia Scott-Clark. The book could use a bit of editing, yet I find it charming and real.

Though not about orbs, Lynn McTaggart's work, *The Intention Experiment,* is one of the works that I'd never want to be without. I have everything she's written on my shelves. Her solid research and attention to scientific fact give the kind of evidence that even the most solid doubters can't logically dispute. It's works like hers that show us how the impossible is just something we've yet to see.

There was a passage in her work that spoke about how Native American tribal people had not panicked at the sight of the first great white sails of ships as they approached. The natives hadn't reacted because they couldn't see the sails in front of their own eyes—those sails were outside any frame of reference they had, so to their eyes they didn't exist. One of the chiefs had finally seen the ships and alerted the others. Once he pointed out the ships, the others could then see them. This curious matter was explained in that what is outside our realm of experience is, in essence, invisible.

I decided I would take an approach to potentially seeing the orbs, becoming, in one sense, my own chief, and because I've never been one to believe I had to be handicapped by what someone else thought was impossible, I reached out with my thoughts to ask orbs to make themselves visible. Knowing that stating the intention was all that was needed, I didn't give my request more thought.

In 2010, sitting in an audience of hundreds listening to Michael Beckwith and John Thurman, I noticed two orbs sharing the stage with the men. My first thought was that this must be the lighting. Then I began to watch with greater focus, seeing where the lights were positioned, looking for possible reflective surfaces, and so on. Perhaps the orbs were aware of my observation, for they played.

Sometimes one would hover over the top of Michael Beckwith's head; at other times they paired up and lay against the drapery background—an area where there certainly was no chance of reflection or the capturing of prisms of light. I noted that the lighting as well as the recording cameras were focused on the speakers and never wavered, yet the orbs moved as they desired. The key element in knowing they were orbs was when one had part of its "body" behind one of the vases gracing the stage. No way was this coming from one of the stage lights positioned in front of Beckwith and Thurman!

The smaller of the orbs would gently fade into my awareness, then out. At times it would come close, getting within a few seats in front of me, then it would travel to another part of the room, then fade out again. Three or four times during the evening, it hovered over Robert Thurman's left shoulder. These orbs gave me quite the performance that evening and I've had orbs in my awareness ever since.

Interestingly enough, whenever I now see Roy Craig, orbs surround him. Inside his home, they will often float in hallways. Their energy around him is one of protection. Sometimes when I see orbs in other settings, it's almost as if they have an air of indifference, as commuters might have as they go to and from their work. Like humans, orbs come in all sizes, though the forms are circular. Colors range, too—at least to my eye—though the differences are generally quite subtle variations on a pale white-gold. I have seen pale pinks and other pastel colors, though not often. They seem to be a benign race, lending energy when they can, as friends would do.

In the time since I first had orbs enter my awareness, I've made efforts to communicate with them. They create what I'd call an "energy wave" that isn't composed of words, it's merely a feeling. In this fashion, they communicate that they are peaceful and are here as observers and, sometimes, protectors.

There have been some amazing photographs and videos taken of orbs. Two places to find pictures and information about orbs as well as information about other alien sightings are www.ecti.org and the Coast to Coast radio show.

While all orbs I've met have "good" energy, just as with anything both in the natural world and the supernatural world, there can be both good and negative energy. Aliens come in both packages, though with orbs, like I mentioned, I've only seen positive energy.

As for seeing orbs with the naked eye, I only had to believe I could and then relax and allow them to make themselves present to me. I believe that it's possible for anyone who believes, or at least is open-minded, to see aliens and other entities once they relax and let the mysteries unfold.

ABOUT TWO-HOUR'S DRIVE from my home is a remarkable place to visit. Nestled in a quiet, lovely valley outside the town of Trout Lake, Washington, you can find ECTI Ranch. Near the base of Mt. Adams, the ranch is renowned as being a location where alien spacecraft can be viewed. I'd wanted for ages to visit but, for one reason or another, hadn't been able to make the trip. When I at last had the opportunity to go, there were forest fires raging and the base of the mountain wasn't even visible because of the smoke. My expectations were low, yet I was already there, so I decided to have a look. I'm so thankful I did!

Just after dusk, I began to see tiny blips of light darting into the top area of the mountain. I hasten to say there are no highways, towns, individual homes, or campsites perched at that high elevation, so there's no way any of the lights could have been from pre-existing sources. On top of that, these lights were coming from the sky and moving towards the mountain.

I began to count the ships. After I'd seen forty, I quit counting. While those were seen as tiny lights, I had the fortune to see one ship close up. It had the typical look one sometimes sees in sci-fi thrillers: an elongated bottom with a bit of a flattened dome on top. Typical or not, I was mesmerized.

I went back about three weeks later. Having seen so much activity the first time, I didn't expect to see as much going on. Looking at the website, I'd seen many pictures of orbs there, so when I got there after dark one evening, the first thing I did was use my camera flash to see what I might see with the naked eye. The orbs I saw went beyond my wildest imagination: thousands floated in the air. I kept flashing the camera to see if anyone else in my party could see them, but they could not. I settled for taking some pictures. While the full thousands can't be seen on the camera, I got, nonetheless, some great pictures of these wonderful beings. Like all the experiences I've had, I love it when there is evidence that even those who question everything can't dispute.

> *Note: Since this time, I returned with a group who took pictures. They are posted at* **www.YourLovingSpirit.com.**

While we didn't get the second experience on film, there were so many spaceships in the sky that night. Those who might say we saw satellites or even aircraft would have a hard time explaining how these craft moved forwards, backwards, and could disappear in a blink of the eye.

If you ever get a chance, you'll want to go to ECTI Ranch yourself. You'll need a private invitation. Here's the website: **www.eceti.org/** In addition to information about the viewings, there is a lot of other information there that I find fascinating.

As with all things "alien" to us, it's easier to believe when you see things for yourself. Begin taking pictures with the intention of "catching" orbs and I think you'll soon discover their presence.

I've posted various orb pictures on my website.

IF YOU'RE INTERESTED IN exploring other things "alien", you may want to check out a series of books that I have on my "most revered" list. They are written by Suzanne Ward.

Suzanne began to channel her son, Matthew, and later, many others we consider alien. There's so much more to these books than just a look at aliens. Starting with *Matthew, Tell Me about Heaven*, they are thought-provoking and fascinating works. I consider them some of the most interesting books I've read.

Suzanne's site, if you're interested, is
http://www.matthewbooks.com
I highly encourage you to read the books before you get into the monthly messages, as the books will give you a foundation.

CHAPTER 20

Ghosts

THE HOUSE HAD BEEN built in the early 1900s, so having a few ghosts around would seem only natural. That wasn't why I was there, however.

A business client who knows the "other side" of what I do asked if I'd see if there was an entity in her house and, if so, clear that energy from her home. She said she'd been feeling for some time that there was something else inside the house with her. Her concern was not only for herself, but for her young son. She knew entities could sometimes inhabit a person—and she wasn't taking any chances.

One of the things that happens for me is that I get a strong sense of these entities "knowing" when I'm connecting to them. Naturally, they don't want to be exposed and have to leave the spots they've inhabited, be that within a person or elsewhere.

This one was no exception, for I felt the entity and knew clearly how to move him out of that space.

That day, as sometimes happens, the entity tried to hide. If some of them weren't so intent on dark ways, their efforts when they do this would be funny. I found the entity and carefully cast him out. Then I made the rounds of the house in order to clear every space in case anything else lurked.

What I found surprised me.

I'd sensed something else around when I'd cleared the entity, yet hadn't been quite able to "see" what it was. Now the game was up, as I could see her clearly.

She began talking as soon as she realized she'd been discovered.

"Please," said the woman, her form when I focused upon her becoming that of a slender elderly woman in a long blue-gray dress, "I won't cause trouble. Please don't make me leave."

My experience with ghosts has been that they usually don't know they're dead. When I work them towards this realization, they want to go to the next realm. This woman didn't want to go anywhere and she knew darn well she was dead. She loved the home and was content to stay put. If allowed. This posed a bit of a dilemma.

I walked back down the stairs where the homeowner awaited.

"The entity is gone," I said. "Now I know this is a bit weird, but there's a ghost here, too, and . . . well, she wants to stay. She promised not to cause any problems. I'll send her on if that's your wish."

To my relief, my client's kind nature ruled.

"No, no," she can stay. "She won't bother me, will she?" she added, needing a bit of reassurance.

"No, she's been here for years and for whatever reason she

likes this space so much she doesn't want to leave. She seems quite happy. I'm glad you'll let her stay. If there's any problem, I'll come back and send her to Light."

The feeling of the ghost-woman's delight when I told her she could stay still makes me smile.

NOT ALL GHOSTS KNOW they are ghosts, nor do they necessarily coexist well with us.

THE CONDO SAT ON a piece of riverfront property that had, long ago, been a space where Native Americans had camped and conducted trade.

Christopher* called me to have me check out his place. He said he hadn't been sleeping well, that it seemed like there was something in the closet in his bedroom. For days, he'd slept on his couch on the lower level of the condo, never going upstairs because of the bad vibes he got when he went up there.

I'd done clearing work for Christopher before and had cast out some seriously nasty entities, including one who had followed him to his car and travelled with him when he went to other homes, so to have him sensing something more in his space was disconcerting.

As soon as I headed up the stairs, I could tell this was something different. I sensed, before I saw, the Native American man. What I realized in moments was that he was as afraid of Christopher as Christopher was of him. I stepped into the Native American man's dimension and saw that the space around him had the elements of his time. There were no condos. His space existed as one where grasses stretched out towards the river and brush housing with hides thrown over the top had been erected to protect from the rain. Strips of salmon, elk, and deer hung above smoking fires and other Native Americans walked about, working on various projects. In this man's mind, he believed evil spirits were after him, for he could sense Christopher and, not seeing him, believed the worst. In his dimension, no closet existed, he sat inside a shelter, wary and on guard.

Why is it that times from the past can sometimes overlap into the current time? How can people like the little old lady ghost know they aren't in a current time and yet others live on in a time warp? I don't know the answer. I only know this exists. Scientists have been postulating for ages that time may fold upon itself rather than run linearly. I can travel back and forth between times that have existed here on earth, but only when there are others to draw me there or when I do a regression or progression, not—so far at least—am I able to go back to a specific time.

Now I had two men, each fearful of the other, both residing in the same space, in different times on earth.

I did what I could think to do and began to create a type of barrier around time, working on the Native American to give him a sense of peace, putting into his thoughts that good spirits surrounded him, that there was nothing to fear. These efforts worked as I'd intended, for I could feel him relax. As that happened, I finished putting the barrier in place. And just like that, he winked away from Christopher's dimension.

I told Christopher what I'd done.

The next morning he called to say he'd been able to sleep in his bed for the first time in days.

SEEING INTO OTHER REALMS is, to state the obvious, fascinating. There's no proof I can offer, of course, that any of what I see of other beings, other worlds, levels of heaven, and so on, even exist.

I choose to share those visions anyway. Some of you will experience that "knowing" inside you that's like the tickle of premonition that is later fulfilled. Others will have had similar experiences. And then there are those of you who will think it's all a bit nuts. That's okay, too.

CHAPTER 21

Akashic Records

LSO CALLED "THE BOOK OF LIFE" throughout the Old and New Testaments, the Records are sometimes referred to as the Celestial Tablets. In addition to information about each soul, they contain great sources of spiritual information.

For anyone not familiar with the Records, they reside in the heavenly realms and hold the information for every soul in all its incarnations from the beginning of time and projecting forward until that soul is eventually reunited with Creator.

Looking into the Akashic Records for someone can be a time-consuming process. In my experience, it's never taken less than a few hours. There are "rules" one has to follow, for opening the Records isn't a game. The messages contained therein are best accessed for deep exploration of life purpose and other primary concerns.

The opportunity to explore the Akashic Records is available to all and can sometimes offer answers that help make this lifetime easier or at least give explanation to things about which we may be confused. While available, access must be approached through humbleness and learned skills and is not to be taken lightly or be used for anything but the most important of purposes.

In accessing the Records, you, or whoever opens the Records for you, will be working with guides and other amazing spiritual beings whose job it is to guard and manage the Records. They decide—not you or the person who opens the Records on your behalf—what you're allowed to know at each stage of your life in each incarnation.

There are limited good books on how to access the Akashic Records, though one that does a good job of guiding through a prayer process is *How to Read the Akashic Records,* by Linda Howe.

At least once in your lifetime, getting a glimpse of what these records have to share with you can be an amazing and humbling experience.

CHAPTER 22

Returning Spirits

'VE HAD SEVERAL LOVELY experiences where souls who are waiting to return to earth have spoken to me. One of these episodes was with two little girls.

A WELL-RESPECTED SPEAKER got off the stage to the sound of much applause. She had made a generous offer to speak with audience members about their businesses in fifteen-minute segments. I hadn't intended to do so, but a friend urged me to talk with her. As much as I'm able, when guided by those who care about me, I honor their requests. I know entities and other beings or souls work through them sometimes to reach me. This was to be one of those times.

Sitting across from Karen* I explained that I didn't have a particular reason or need to meet with her. Her eyebrows rose in surprise. I'm sure most of the people that day had well-thought-out plans on how this vivacious, intelligent woman could help them and had delved right in to ask questions as soon as they could.

"Well, tell me what you do," said Karen.

In that moment, I knew the meeting with her wasn't about me at all. The messages for her began to come in. After letting her know the kind of work I do in the spirit realm, I asked her permission to share the information I was receiving. The remainder of the fifteen minutes consisted of me delivering a steady stream of messages. She sat back, aghast. "No one knows about this," she said at one point. Then, "I can't believe this is happening." People were lining up in the waiting area and she seemed a bit flustered that our time had gone so quickly.

She reached out and took my hand. "I have to stay on schedule, but I want to talk to you more if you're willing."

I told her I was, and that I'd be around until two o'clock, then needed to catch a flight.

When I'd been back and forth to the meeting room, I'd caught her eye several times but she'd been busy with consultations. Comfortable that we'd meet up again, I went to get my luggage. As soon as she saw me with suitcases, she beckoned. She clearly was in the middle of a consultation with two women, yet I realized she was afraid she wouldn't be able to catch me again. She apologized to them, saying she'd only be a minute. Drawing me aside, she asked if I'd seen anything more.

I had. What I hadn't known was that she'd been trying to

get pregnant. I told her there were two little girls coming in. At this, she drew her breath in and I watched as she struggled to keep her professional demeanor. Even so, I saw tears form in the corners of her eyes.

"I'm tied up here," she said, "but may I email you?" She slipped me her card and I gave her mine.

"Of course," I said. Little did I know that the children coming in for her would fill my head with their chatter for days.

Here's an excerpt of our email exchanges, with deletions to keep identifying factors private:

> *"Those girls of yours are real chatterboxes. Ever since I let them in, it's like they can't stop themselves, their excitement is so great. It's as if they've already formed from spirit into a place that's halfway between that realm and the realm of substance. Usually I can't see form with those coming into the world, but I can almost see these two—it's rather like seeing them through translucent curtains. In the vision, they are about 5 and 6, slender little blue-eyed blondes, though one is a darker blonde. Their little bodies remind me of colts, all bones and awkwardness, like they're trying to figure out how they are supposed to work these bodies. They bicker (in a sweet way) about whether or not they want to be girls, who gets to come in first, and so on. They have been together in many lifetimes and they agree this one is special because they will be with you again. Be prepared, as they are quite the teasers and have great fun with their innocent mischievousness.*
>
> *I just wanted you to know that they are excited*

and they gave a lot of thought to choosing you. Even as I write this, they are saying, "she's getting ready!" I'm letting them know I've told you so they will quiet down.

Karen responded, saying she'd gotten chills when she read my note, as she'd always felt she had a five or six-year-old "out there" somewhere. She said she and her husband had been taking classes to increase their chances of getting pregnant.

Here is part of the response I emailed to her:

Just so you know, you don't need a class to get pregnant ;-) They ARE coming in. I hear their sweet little giggles even as I write this. Don't be too surprised if these little teases show up as brown-eyed boys, because that's the mischievous energy they have! They don't want anyone knowing all their secrets. The one thing that's real clear is that they will be inseparable. They will love you in this lifetime as they have in the past. Oh my goodness. Just got a huge hit on why they are showing up at that age. I've got chills all over my body. I'm hesitant to say this in an email, but I'm going to anyway, as I think you'll want to know right away and may not have a chance to call me. In their immediate past life you were their mother then, too. They drowned in a canal near your home. I'm getting Holland or somewhere like that. The ages I see them at right now are the ages they were when they passed. I see a steep bank on the edge of a canal. It's covered with long grasses and the grass is slick. The younger one slid on the grass and she fell into the canal. Her sister tried to go after her and fell in too. Neither of them could get out. They are telling you that it wasn't your fault, saying now you know you weren't to blame, so you don't have to keep them away. They say they knew they were supposed to stay near the house and that they love you very much and wanted to make sure they came back to you. They are also telling you not to worry, that they will be okay this time. They say they hesitated to come back to you because they didn't want you to be afraid for them all the time but they decided together that they must be with you once more.

Wow. What a download. Holy cow, but I'm still taken aback sometimes. No wonder you say you feel like you have a 5 or 6-year old out there. These girls have been around you.

For roughly two weeks, the girls were almost constantly chattering in my head. Although I'd seen it for myself, they kept explaining they'd been with Karen in, what sounded to me, like Holland. They weren't sure, though they were eager to give descriptions of everything remembered: they had lived on a farm and there were big canals (they actually described them as slow, wide waters, which I translated into being canals) that ran around the fields. Karen, as their mother in that past life, had told them not to play by the water, they said. The youngest girl wanted to see what was out there and why her mother thought it was so dangerous. Her sister followed, a bit later, concerned their mother would catch them and they'd be in trouble.

The youngest sister found herself at the edge of the canal. Here is how they both told me about their death:

"The grass was long and wet. I felt myself sliding on the grass and into the water I went. The water was cold and I didn't know how to swim. I went under the water and then came up again and saw Sister. Sister lay on her belly and held out her hand to grab me and pull me out. I grabbed hard, because I was so afraid and there was water in my mouth. Sister slid, too, and came in on top of me. We both went under the water." She paused for a minute and then said, *"Angels helped us. We weren't afraid anymore."*

The older sister spoke up, "Except for Mama and Papa being sad, dying wasn't so bad. Actually, it was nice."

The younger one giggled. "Now we're coming back. We get to come back any way we want. I think I want to be a boy."

"No you don't," said the older sister. "You told me we'd be girls again, only this time you wanted to be the older sister."

They went on squabbling, just as siblings in this dimension do. The trouble was, they squabbled for days on end, reciting little memories of the mama they planned to come back to, making plans for what they wanted to do when they grew up this time, and more. It became too much. At last I had to call a halt to their communications, telling them they could talk with me if it was really important—and only then.

OFTEN EXPERIENCES WE HAVE in this life are related to what has happened in past lives. Karen's fear of losing the girls she'd lost before had caused her to keep from getting pregnant in this lifetime. At a level she couldn't quite grasp, the possibility of losing them again was just too much to handle. Now that she has the awareness of what happened, she can let down her guard and allow the children to come in. Knowledge of many-lifetime connections can be healing and sometimes provide blessings in many areas of our lives.

CHAPTER 23

Messages Of Love

OFTEN, THE PEOPLE WHO come to me are referred from friends or those I've helped. This was the case with Sarah*.

A mutual friend had mentioned her. I'd worked with him and he knew I might be able to help Sarah quit smoking. She called, asking if I'd mind making a house call. Since she was living close by, I agreed to do so. The mutual friend hadn't told me much about her, other than what a good person she was and how he thought she could use my help.

Meeting Sarah, her warmth and kindness were evident. As psychics, there are people we meet who just have a special energy of goodness around them and Sarah had this energy in spades. After exchanging some small talk, I began to work with her on the smoking issue.

My attention pulled away and I looked into the room near us. As I did, a scene unfolded before me. While it hadn't been my intention, nor had it been Sarah's when she'd called me, when I receive messages I pass them on. Having been blessed to be a conduit, I don't take the responsibility lightly.

"Sarah, I am seeing someone who wants to talk to you. Are you okay with that?"

"Absolutely," she said, "who is it?"

"I'm seeing a young man, not quite a teenager. His hair is dark and so are his eyes. His complexion is on the darker side. He's wearing a baseball cap and he's got a mitt on. He's bouncing a ball up and down in the mitt. He's in the middle of a flat, grassy, field-like area and there are tall pines all around the edge of this big expanse."

Staring into that other place as I immersed myself into communication with this boy, I hadn't been observing Sarah. She let out a wrenching sob that caused me to turn to look at her. Tears gushed down her face.

"Oh, my God!" said Sarah. "That's my son! He was killed when he was twelve. Please tell me what he's saying," she begged.

"He's saying, 'It's not your fault, Mom. You couldn't help what happened. I'm happy and I'm always with you.' "

Torturous sobs wracked her. I moved towards her and wrapped my arms around her shuddering body. I held her until she finally sobbed out the old grief.

She pushed away from my shoulder. "Can I see him if I try?"

"I can't say for sure, but I think now that you've connected, that might happen. He loves you so much and wants you to realize he's never left you. Even if you don't see him, he's always around."

Sarah grabbed a box of tissues and blew her nose. "I've thought sometimes that he was, kind of like, watching me. I didn't know if what I thought I saw was real."

"He's always been there," I assured her.

At that moment, a woman's image appeared before me.

"I'm seeing someone else who wants to give you a message, Sarah."

She nodded her permission.

"This woman is taking me back in time. I see her rushing, saying, 'hurry, hurry,' and you're with her. I think this must be your mom. There's someone else there, too. I think it's a female, younger than you. Do you have a younger sister?" I didn't wait for an answer, as the woman's energy felt too urgent. "The woman is holding you both by your hands, pulling you along. You're all running from someone."

Sarah began rocking back and forth, sobbing even more, trying to handle what had just happened. Minutes passed before she finally gained control. She began to share her story. Her father had been physically abusive and her mother had feared for the safety of Sarah and her younger sister. Although Sarah had been too young to remember, she had learned that as her mother was escaping with them, Sarah's father had chased after them and shot and killed her mother.

"Why is she here?" Sarah whimpered.

"She has a message for you."

"Oh God, oh God, I don't know if I can do this," said Sarah.

"I'll share only if you want me to," I said.

"Yes, tell me." Sarah took a deep breath and seemed to gird herself.

"Your mother tells me she gave her life because she knew

you had something important to accomplish. She wants you to know that by not taking care of yourself you're not able to live your purpose. She also says you don't have to be strong alone, that she forever walks with you."

As Sarah cried again, the medical intuitive part of me fired up and I could see what Sarah's mother was talking about when she spoke about Sarah not taking care of herself.

"You already know your smoking is a problem. I see your lungs filling up." I paused for a moment, unsure of just how to tell her what else I saw. Taking a deep breath, I said, "If you don't quit smoking, soon it will be too late. You'll never recover your health. I'll help you, but you need to know there's a small window of time for you to get healthy before irrevocable disease sets in. I'm seeing your lungs as if they are two oblong containers. They are half-filled with darkness." I paused for a bit as more information flowed in. "Have you been having pain in the area of your liver?"

Sarah's eyes widened. She told me she had.

Once more, I paused. "Have you been drinking a lot?"

At this point I think Sarah realized there wasn't any reason to hide anything from me.

"I've just felt so empty inside. Nothing seems to work and I don't know where to turn. I've blamed myself, too, for my son dying." She cried again and once more I held her.

"You know he doesn't blame you," I soothed. "You're the only one who's ever set blame."

"If I drink, I can forget for a while."

"That has to stop. Remember what your mother said?"

Sarah wiped at her tears. "She believes in me, doesn't she?"

"Yes. So what is it you're supposed to be doing?"

"I don't know."

"You do. You haven't given yourself permission to believe you can do this yet."

"I'm supposed to help other parents who've lost children, aren't I?"

I smiled at her, delighted she saw this so clearly. "Your mom is smiling at me, nodding her head."

A big smile lit her face, flowing joy into the core of her. Her spirit shined.

"Now let's work at getting you healthy again."

CHAPTER 24

Past Lives

THE NOTION THAT WE'VE lived more than one life had always been something I scoffed at. I felt people who held that notion were living in a fantasy, a sort of escape from their present life at best. At worst, I thought they sought an excuse for behavior they could blame on something other than their lack of willpower.

Interesting, isn't it, how perspectives can change with experience?

Somewhere in my early teens, my grandmother had asked me to clean and clear a linen closet. I began by taking everything off the shelves, stacking linens and other materials on a bed so I could sort and fold. As I neared the bottom of the lowest shelf, I saw there were old sepia-colored photographs, roughly 17" x 25" in size. They lay there, at the bottom of the stack, probably placed there to protect the surfaces. Pulling them out, I saw the first was one of a man who was probably in his forties. The second was of a woman of roughly the same age. When I pulled the last picture out, I felt my throat tighten. I looked into the face of a young woman, who bore a rather stern countenance and was probably in her late twenties when the picture had been taken. There was no resemblance that I could see, nor do I remember anything of that lifetime. All I knew then, and am just as sure of now, is that this picture reflected me..

After realizing this, I began to look at the many studies done. Most reputable are those of Dr. Ian Stevenson.

On the website **www.reluctant-messenger.com**, an article about Stevenson, written by *OMNI Magazine* correspondent Meryle Secrest some years ago, says this:

> *Since the late Sixties Dr. Ian Stevenson, Carlson Professor of Psychiatry and Director of the Division of Personality Studies at the University of Virginia, has documented cases in India, Africa, the Near and Far East, Britain, the United States, and elsewhere in which young children have astonished their parents with precise details about the people they claim to have been. Some of these children have recognized former homes and neighborhoods as well as still-living friends and relatives. They have recalled events in their purported previous lives, including their often violent deaths. Sometimes their birthmarks resemble scars that correspond to wounds that led, they claim, to their deaths.*
>
> *Dr. Stevenson has devoted the last forty*

imagination and I hungered to see what awaited.

Suddenly the journey stopped and I could see myself in a past life. Later, Ralph said perhaps I'd gone to Lemuria or Atlantis, yet I never had the feeling that was the setting. Instead, the place felt like a place currently undiscovered.

Beneath my feet, sands of blues, purples and greens, shifted—living energies of their own. I was working in what we'd describe as a lab, though the elements I worked with weren't of any known substance, save that of crystals which were being used along with these substances. I was female and my clothing floated about me in diaphanous waves bearing the same colors as the sands, only with pinks and radiant golden threads worked into the fabric.

My features were human and the form they took was of a woman in what we'd think of as her 20s or 30s. This "other me" had hair that fell in gentle golden curls to her waist and, while she was quite tall, her features were delicate and beautiful. The scene shifted and I saw myself being awarded by a council of elders for a discovery I had made around healing. Just as I saw this, I saw another woman and felt her deep hatred.

The woman was older, her facial features angular, her hair in unruly tight curls, her form not as pleasing to the eye as the form I then possessed. She had made the same discovery as I had and, she believed, the recognition had been awarded me because of my looks when she should have been recognized as well. All of this was delivered to me in a form of knowing, just as I knew she would later kill me from her festering hatred.

I'd seen enough.

Ralph had been asking me what I was seeing, but I'd kept the experience to myself. He brought me back.

"Wow," I said. "I can't believe I went back the way I did."

I shook my shoulders out, the clarity of the images still with me. "It scared me a bit about how fast I travelled." I went on to explain how I felt as if each ridge I passed through in the tunnel took me through tens, then hundreds, of years at a time.

Up until that time, I hadn't paid attention to my friend who'd asked if she could sit and observe. She spoke up.

"I think I went with you," she said. She went on to describe all the things I hadn't spoken about, describing how I appeared, what the area around me looked like, what I'd been doing. Then, even more eerily, she described the other woman, though she had no sense of what the woman had been thinking or of the deep hatred that woman had for me.

Sometimes I have to be hit over the head with evidence in order to believe. For, despite my experience of seeing the "past me" in that picture from my grandmother's linen closet, I hadn't fully accepted the idea of past lives.

For days afterward, I pondered what I might have needed to learn from that time. It's my belief (which I've since substantiated from journeys into the Akashic Records) that we have something we're supposed to learn in each lifetime and a role we're supposed to play for others in their own journeys of learning. I realized I knew the other woman. She is in this lifetime. My struggles with her have been similar in that I feel she has always felt she is in competition with me. Her resentment at times has had a depth to it that didn't make sense until I saw how this hatred had carried forward from eons ago. I use this knowledge now to give her recognition whenever I have the opportunity, going out of my way to say genuine, kind things about her intelligence, her talents. The softening of her attitude towards me has been remarkable.

Though the Council of that time had given me recognition

and I hadn't sought the attention for myself, that didn't matter. What mattered was that the element of hatred had an energy that had never dissipated. I believe the knowledge of this past life helps me to diffuse the bad energy and create a healing that would otherwise perhaps carry forward to other lifetimes. Learning how the past-life regression benefitted me gave me reason to help others through assisting them in taking their own journeys back in time.

Since the time of learning how to go back in time, I've had opportunity to see how others do regressions. Often, the person doing the regression doesn't fully trust their process, so they plant leading questions. Even though I put my hand on the shoulder of the person I'm regressing and, quite often, go with them on their journey, I don't mention the things I see other than to say, perhaps, something innocuous such as "I see a path" or "do you want to take this road?", and then I ask the person if they'd like to see where that leads.

Trust that you'll know when the experiences are real ones. Know, too, that when you take these journeys you're allowed to do so because there's something to learn that will benefit you in the journey you are on inside this lifetime.

CHAPTER 25

Future Lives

THE EXPERIENCE OF TRAVELLING to past lives became comfortable. The more I did this, the more I wondered about how time worked.

Amit Goswami in his book *Physics of the Soul* shares how Einstein had an interesting perspective on death. "He maintained that past, present, and future all exist at some level, simultaneously." Goswami shared this comment from Einstein, too: "For we convinced physicists, the distinction between past, present, and future is only an illusion."

If time had the sort of fluidity that I imagined it to have, I reasoned, couldn't we move *forward* significantly in time? I'd already experienced seeing into the future with many predictions becoming true, so why would there be a cut-off point? Why couldn't we see beyond this lifetime?

Once more, I called on my friend Ralph. I told him what I wanted him to do. By now, I'd become adept at past-life regression. I didn't know what to expect with what I planned, I just believed "transporting" into the distant future was possible.

This time, I travelled through a tunnel, too. The experience wasn't the same, however, for the rings I passed through didn't have the same drag to them. They felt lighter, not as tight. Travelling back in time for me always has the sensation of being pulled through the rings with an almost sucking sensation.

Soon, I emerged into the future time I was meant to experience. A slight hill rose in the distance. Walking towards the hill, there lay before me a grove of beings. Their bases were anchored as trees would be on this plane, yet the "branches" were more like tentacles, and they were transparent as jellyfish. I knew immediately they were my elders and that they formed a part of my soul's guidance system, determining in each lifetime if I was following a path of learning that would ultimately, through many lifetimes, connect me at the highest level with God. Each being shimmered with a different color, one blue, one violet, one emerald, one the color of sunshine, another orange, one rose, and one turquoise. Tentacle-branches undulated in the air and slipped in and out of slight color variances as if gentled into color-shifting by the wind.

I felt their wisdom.

"You're on the right path," they whisper-talked into my consciousness. "Your path is always to be one of healer." I felt their great acceptance-oneness-love to the core of me, an embracing completeness of profound sweetness. Then, just as quickly as they had embraced me, they let me go.

I journeyed back.

While I can't prove this experience was real in the same way that having someone "see" the same things I saw in my past-life exploration does, the experience felt real.

I like to remember those sentient beings as guardians of my soul journey. I find it fitting they are anchored, yet their flow of thought is never contained to one space. They are but one form of "alien" life I've seen. Just as those other forms have come into my experience, I know we are all connected, all Creator's loved ones.

THE DIFFERENCES I'VE SEEN with past-life regression versus what I've dubbed future-life progression are that with most future-life work there will be two or three paths ahead. Clearly, we are taking our lives forward with choice as our companion. The power of that *choice*, as I see it, is what helps us progress more quickly (or not) to elevations of enlightenment.

CHAPTER 26

Religion

'VE HAD ISSUE WITH some of the beliefs and things I see happening that come from what I call "traditional" religion. This doesn't mean every religion is bad— far from it—however there is enough perpetuation of bad and even evil advice given out by those who claim religious "authority" who are creating horrible injustices in the name of God that I want to address those injustices here to the best of my ability. Why? Because as I've immersed myself deeper into the psychic realm, the connection to the universal energy I call God has gotten even more profound and I believe if those of us who do our best to teach about goodness don't have at least as strong a voice as those who teach wrong thinking, then we are not doing the work we're here to do.

If you are one who has been gifted with the ability to connect to Source energy quickly (we all have this ability, but at this time, few are exercising this connection), then you've been given that ability so you can help be a voice on earth. *All* are supposed to be speaking out for goodness and love, so if you haven't been doing so, don't leave that up to someone else, even if you don't consider yourself psychic.

There are four messages that stand out for me. I don't claim they came in one big psychic revelation: they are messages that came over time, reinforced over and over again by Creator. I've condensed them into a format that seems to best represent the total of them.

1. **God is love.** Not love only for a certain denomination, a given color of skin, a sexual orientation, or only for those who are sprinkled or immersed in water (though He appreciates our willingness to have greater connection with Him). He loves the sinner and the saint equally.

   As a Sunday School teacher, there was a little song I had all the children sing, and if you ever attended church as a child, it's likely you sang the same verses:

   > *"Jesus loves the little children,*
   > *All the children of the world;*
   > *Red and yellow, black and white,*
   > *All are precious in his sight;*
   > *Jesus loves the little children of the world."*

   If we added the words "and God" next to "Jesus" that is a nice summary of how these almighty ones love: they love all of us, regardless of color or anything else.

When we get into the spirit of judging others, this is the furthest we get from living in the Holy Spirit, the furthest from doing the work of God. When those who enter into a mode of thinking wherein they are judging others or thinking they are for some reason more beloved than someone else, it is then that they are instead embracing the heart of darkness, for this is the kind of energy that the dark ones would have us reside inside. Just as the little verse depicts love for all children, so too are we all, and I emphasize all, the children of God.

God's command is simple: **Be love in the world.** Just so you know, the prophet Jesus is one of many prophets—don't get hung up on the notion that one prophet is more important to God than another. When you have issue with any of this remember: God is love. If you come back to that dictum whenever you have a decision-point in your life and you try to live as God-like as you can, you will lead a life of goodness and be closer to the union with God.

2. **Our Creator doesn't care what you call Him.** I use the name God, but those are only letters on a page or a sound issued from my mouth. What matters is the energy behind my thoughts and intentions. For anyone to defile the names that others use for our Creator is to belittle Him (or Her, if you prefer). God overlooks so many of our human misunderstandings. Ultimately we will see that we all worship the same Creator. Having said this, we know we're worshipping the same God if we see Him as a God of peace, love, and kindness—for all. Anything less is worshipping the dark one or at the very least planting seeds that allow the dark one to take root and grow larger in our being. If

you're following someone who tells you that others are less than you or that others have less of a connection to God, I urge you to start thinking independently with the soul (and brain and heart) God gave you and seek to examine the true meanings of godliness.

3. **Your connection to God is a direct one.** You don't need a priest, a minister, a mullah, a rabbi, or any other denominational leader or person to talk to God on your behalf. Those who do their best to deceive you into thinking you have to go through them to be forgiven, to be blessed, etc., will have that to deal with in another of their lifetimes. All you need to do to connect to God is be in meditation, prayer, or simply ask for that presence. The connections are strengthened over time in a way similar to how we build strength in a muscle.

   If you want a connection with Creator, you have that connection easily available. You don't have to pay anyone, go to a particular building, etc. If the place you go to is a place where you feel peaceful and centered and your gifts are given freely there so that they may help others, that's a good place. I'd say if that's your practice, keep it up. Don't forget, however, that connecting to Creator on a regular basis, not just once a week or even once a day, is what you want to practice. I do my best to connect every morning and evening and have little "check-ins" throughout the day. Loving God is an action, not a philosophy.

4. **Hell is of our own making.** That doesn't mean that some souls won't go to what we call hell, but those are the souls that have intentionally chosen evil and want to reside in a

place of darkness. All of us have done things we wish we hadn't. Here's where the true meaning of *karma* comes in: *karma* means if we make bad choices and take bad actions and don't acknowledge those as being bad and then choose to live differently, we have to have the experience of that same choice being presented in another lifetime.

Sometimes in that next life we're the victim of someone else doing that bad thing to us so we can see what that felt like; at other times we're given that same experience again so we will have a chance to make a better choice. *Karma*, simplified in my humble attempt to explain, is this: each lifetime offers choices.

Good choices mean you move up in the hierarchy of spirit-growth to grow closer to Creator. Bad choices mean you stay where you're at until you make better choices.

Those for whom there are no future lifetimes where they can move closer to God are those who deliberately choose to draw in evil and then enjoy that connection with darkness so much that they never regret the evil they perpetuate. When they die, they do not move forward into another lifetime, they go to what we call "hell" which is a place where those of the same evil persuasion perpetuate upon each other those deeds that they have grown to covet. If these souls come forward into our world again, they do so in the form of demons.

CHAPTER 27

Healing

AMONG THE MANY EXPERIENCES I've had since healing myself so many years ago are times when I've been blessed to be able to minister to others who have had diagnoses such as Parkinson's disease, kidney failure, tumor masses and other ailments and diseases. These healings are what we call miracles, yet I rush to assure you, the performance of "miracles" is not the dominion of a few.

Throughout our time on earth, there have been stories of medical miracles and many other situations that we refer to as miracles. I say "that we refer to as miracles" because I believe miracles are only those things we do not yet see as possible.

In Brazil, João de Deus, or John of God, performs many

miracles every day, from multiple surgeries with bare hands or only the crudest of tools, to healing psychological wounds. He's been filmed and studied and deemed legitimate by many doctors, among them the United States television star known as Dr. Oz (who, in addition to being a popular figure on TV is a legitimate physician).

Many thousands have witnessed John of God's visible surgeries, done without anesthetics. He also does many psychic surgeries. The difference, he says, is that some people need to see the physical in order to believe they have been healed. In all his healing work, John of God has other entities working with him. He knows (and it's said his closest assistants know, too) which entity is present when the work is being done, though John of God says all healing is "God, not me."

Thousands of people a year travel to Casa Dom Inacio in Abadiania, Brazil to experience healing and support the work of this great healer-medium. Among those who have experienced healing is spiritual teacher Wayne Dyer, who had been diagnosed with leukemia. Unlike many who travel to Brazil for healing, Wayne Dyer experienced remote healing, which is healing done when the person being worked on is miles, sometimes continents away, from the person who is performing the healing. Archived on Oprah.com is the experience Dyer shared with Oprah, as is her own journey and experience.

> Note: Since the first edition of this book, Dr. Wayne Dyer has passed, however he lived until age seventy-five without the pain leukemia traditionally brings.

Like John of God, I harness the power of holy beings and

have them work through me. Also like John of God, I am not a doctor, I am simply a spiritual conduit who connects with the spirits of others so they can embrace their own healing with my assistance and the assistance of the blessed entities that flow in to provide support.

While John of God practices the Catholic faith, he heals *all* who come, regardless of denomination, or any other label.

I believe in God and Jesus, but I also believe that those are simply names for the great power and wisdom of two higher beings who are Creator energy. In other words, I could call them by any name and my name for them would not change them in any way. They are constant and pure and independent of our human titles. All who worship a Creator who espouses love, whatever they call Him or Her, are worshiping the same great being I call and worship as God. Because of this, I don't adhere to any single religion as a minister—I believe the practice of love embodies all.

I can't speak for John of God, so I will tell you that when I do healing work, the guides (I also call them entities) I use come through me to provide the knowledge I'm lacking. At the same time, my own energy, an energy from before incarnation here on earth, is fully part of the healing ability I tap into. We *all* have the ability to heal ourselves and others. My own faith rests in what I have seen with my own eyes and experienced in my body. I've seen firsthand the transformations that can occur with others. Joined with those experiences is my belief in the biblical edict where Jesus tells us that not only will we be able to do the works He did, but even greater works. Indeed, He proclaims we can move mountains.

I believe as we evolve on this planet, we are only now beginning to step into our power.

As I've been asked by many to describe what happens when I do healing work, I'll share what my experience feels like. I must add that there's no prescribed way for any of us to do healing work, that you may find a way of your own. Unless you are a minister, rabbi, or other licensed spiritual leader or physician, remember that current laws in the United States and many other countries prevent you from doing healing work. Even as a licensed minister, I make sure everyone I work with has traditional medical doctors whom they've seen prior to coming to me.

Before I begin healing work (or any type of spiritual work) I do what I've described as "lining up." This is a combination of prayer and meditation, where I wait until I feel filled up with holy energy. "Filled up" means I can feel energy flowing through my body, especially, though not exclusively, through to my hands and from the area surrounding my heart and solar plexus. At times the energy is so intense my body trembles. In the prayers that accompany my meditation, I ask that whatever healing is needed be done. I do not hold expectations that I can necessarily see everything, despite my attempts to do so, nor do I believe that all healing can be done—sometimes our soul contracts are such that we are meant to experience disharmony in our bodies. My own experience of great pain, for example, gave me the enormous gift of being able to see and help others in ways I'd never imagined previously.

I trust my guides to help me see those times I am allowed to influence self-healing.

After my lining-up process, I can either do hands-on or remote energy work. It's often rather fun for me to do hands-on work, as my hands are guided to the areas where they will have most immediate effect. More often than not, there are areas in the head or feet (or both) where I can work to bring harmony into the body. It's interesting to me that when I'm guided to an area to use healing touch, the person I'm working on will sometimes experience minor pain as I target a distinct spot. That always feels like a verification to these individuals, because I haven't let them point to a specific spot in advance. My psychic abilities will often let me know of other spiritual healing that needs to take place and when that work is necessary, tears often flow as I tap into old wounds that need to be mended before physical healing can begin.

During remote work, I can send healing energy either while the person is on the phone or while they are doing other things. I always check in with people after I've done the work. Almost everyone says they experienced tingling or even some sharp, brief sensations while I was working. Universal is the report from individuals that they are tired after being worked on— and that's for either remote or in-person healing. Any time our bodies experience change, I see rest as a necessary element for the changes to settle in.

Healing work can take place within minutes or it can take me several days or even months. Undoing disease and imbalances (I prefer to think of this as body disharmony) isn't something that happens at a fast pace. Remember, it took time for that disharmony to occur, so it is logical that some time may be necessary for the body to get back into harmony.

When healing does happen within a brief time, even minutes, I'm always delighted and surprised. Why such accelerated healing can occur is only speculation on my part, but I suspect there are those who are so lined up in their own bodies and ready to heal that they simply do so with ease.

I have seen instances where a person has past-life issues

that hold them back from healing. When I tap into these lifetimes and see where a person has "stuck" energy, I can go in and do a clearing that then makes healing available.

Unfortunately, there are never any guarantees that healing can take place. What I hope you will hear is that you need to be careful of anyone who gives an absolute promise that healing can be done, or anyone who charges enormous fees for doing so. It is reasonable to expect that an energy worker charge an hourly fee similar to that of a doctor. Remember that the healer has prep time and a cleansing time afterwards, so that adds as much as an hour either side of the actual energy work. Spiritual healers need to earn a living just like all others who provide their services and talents. The beauty of spiritual healing is there are no long-term drug costs or side-effects.

The best of all scenarios is that you learn how to line up and heal yourself!

IN THE END, IT matters not that I am a seer, for each person needs to learn they are creators of their own journey.

It matters not that I am a healer, for each person needs to learn the power within that allows them to be the healer.

My time will pass, yet the consciousness I embrace will remain a thread in the unified fabric of all that is.

So, if my time will pass—and it will—what is my purpose? My purpose is to lift up to greater understanding those who are still journeying to greater consciousness, just as the purpose of those "above" me in consciousness have the responsibility of lifting me and others like me into greater awareness.

The attainment of wisdom, of connectedness—that is my charge. It is yours as well.

CHAPTER 28

From My Heart

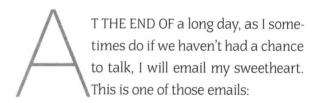T THE END OF a long day, as I sometimes do if we haven't had a chance to talk, I will email my sweetheart. This is one of those emails:

I didn't have a chance to share the sweetest part of my day with you. The young girl I've been working with to contain the tumor had surgery on Wednesday. Her mom had time to write yesterday and in her email she said both doctors used these words: "It's a miracle this tumor didn't affect the ovary. We can't explain it." That made my heart sing.

All my days aren't like that, by any stretch. I give thanks over and over when the powers of assorted heavenly forces flow through me so I can serve others in some way.

You can feel the same way, too.

We all have gifts to share. Too many think *receiving* love and adoration is the goal. They do all they can think of to be the receiver: giving with the expectation of getting; spending small fortunes on facelifts or special trainers in the hope that they will be more desirable; or they think they need to drive a certain kind of car or have a certain amount of money in the bank—all with the expectation that if they *do* a certain thing, possess certain things, or look a certain way they will then be more lovable. They miss the greatest gift available, and it's available instantly with no work, no cost at all: giving love.

You don't have to be psychic to know that the difference you can make on earth is to be loving to others.

Be love. Especially when it's not easy.

You'll fail at this sometimes, I know I do, especially when I get into fear-energy about something. Funny enough, whatever my fears are, rarely do they manifest in a way that's bigger than the fear itself.

I'm still in the process of accepting with grace that sometimes things that are challenging, even situations that I am in despair about, are gifts given for my learning. There is— though sometimes it takes a while to get there—always light ahead.

It's my goal to live in Divine Light. Most of the time, I do pretty well. When I have that perfected, I'll be on the other side of the veil, so I'll be content right now to do the best I can. If you try to do that, too, living in the Light makes life sweet.

I'm often asked questions like "how can I connect with my guides" and "can you teach me to do what you do?" The answers are complex, as they vary from person to person and most things I do are tailored to respect individuality. The one thing I can say with surety is that if you live by letting love flow through you, it won't be long before your feel the companionship of spiritual energies and loving beings.

In reading this work, I hope you will see how much more there is to you, that you'll feel, too, the great continued expansion of all that you are—all that we *all* are—unfolding even as you read these words.

The Universe, Creator, and all the spiritual beings within have this message for you: Always, you are loved.

My love to you, too.

CHAPTER 29

A Final Word From God

THIS IS PURELY WHAT I imagine God would say. I like to think of Creator as being fun, wise, and always looking to expand our thinking and His presence.

HEY, PEEPS, GOD HERE. (I've been waiting to say that for more millenniums than you can wrap your brain around.) Yes, you're all my people, regardless of the name you use: Rama, Akal Purakh, Allah, Yahweh, Jehovah or even (and I have to say I get a kick out of this one: Mother Nature—lovin' that). I don't care much what you call me, though a

whole lot of you get up in arms about the choices of others. That's a pity, but you'll learn that soon enough.

For now, I'll just say I'm a bit disappointed in some of you who have put so much into turning what should have been the honoring of me into a hateful thing. I'm about love, acceptance, kindness and all those things I helped you create within yourselves to make not only your life better, but the lives of others better as well. Guess what? <u>That's</u> what you do to honor me. Nix on the fighting, judging of others, and all sorts of ugliness.

This non-interference decision I made . . . well, sometimes I wonder if I took giving you free will a bit too far, but then I always come back to the same decision when I think this out. I want you to be better people because you want to be better, not because I want that for you. Have to say, though, I've got an ace in the hole. If you're, say, a little lacking in the compassion department, I'll just spit you back out and make you live more lifetimes until you eventually get it right. The downside for some of you is this: I let you be on the other end of the abuse and destruction once in a while. Amazing how that changes perspectives.

Maybe you can tell by now, I'm a pretty fun guy. If I wasn't, would I be saying "hey there" in a book written by a psychic? See, I know ('cause I know all things) there are some of you who think this psychic bit isn't real. I'm a bit dismayed, frankly, because I gave all of you the power to connect with me, and everything in the universe, long ago. I understand that some who call themselves religious leaders try to take this power away from you. Some of you smart ones decided you didn't need to go through others to talk to me. That was cool. Others will come to learn that soon (or I'll do the 'kick 'em back and make them start over' thing).

I gave all of you incredible powers. Pretty mind-blowing, if you ask me, and rather generous if I do say so myself. You only need to learn how to tap into those powers. You know what else? I created lots of other beings who have powers, too . . . oh, wait, seriously now, you didn't think I only created <u>you</u>? I do get some chuckles from you humans.

So the other beings this psychic talks to— they're just more of my creations. Like you humans, there are good ones, bad ones, and real bad ones. (Free-will in evidence.) That's why you always have to use your noggins and protect yourself from evil. I'm always around to help you with that, if you ask.

Oh, I don't want to forget to address this thing about psychic powers and how some of you think those powers aren't real, or are, somehow, evil to use. Those of you who think that believe at the same time in prophets. You know, guys like Isaiah, Jeremiah, Ezekiel, Elisha, Zachariah, Moses. Hello down there! The word prophet comes from prophesize, which means "to see." Ever consider that maybe some of those who wanted power (and your money) might have said anyone who could see things (other than them, of course, 'cause they *claim <u>they</u> can see and are <u>told</u> what is right or wrong) was evil? You might want to think about that if the idea of a psychic gives you heart pains. And incidentally, I don't need anyone to collect money for me. I'm doing just fine. Spend your money directly on helping others. Oh, need to say this, money is only the core of evil when you covet money above people.*

So maybe I got a bit far afield with my message. Forgive me (how do you like that twist?) I do like to go on when I have an audience. Here's the main thing . . . I'll make this a whole lot simpler than the Bible, Koran, or any of the other books people abuse in my name:

- *be kind*
- *judge not others (had to get some of that declaration-type language in here so you'd know it's really me)*
- *don't be greedy, however it's okay to want abundance, because there's abundance enough for all*
- *respect others*
- *be forgiving*
- *have compassion*
- *think for yourself*

I kinda like the idea of seven commandments. If I added one more, I'd say be good to the earth (she's a living entity just like you).

*That final commandment, the one where I tell
you to think for yourself? I've decided it's time you
all had a bit of awareness of both your own power
and of the things outside yourself that so many of
you have kept a blind eye to all this time.*

I'll be around if you need me.

> *Ta-ta for now!*
> *God*

Yes, that's what I'd like to think God would say. In my heart,
I always see Him as the most loving of fathers, one who desires
that we have joy and laughter in our lives.

CHAPTER 30

Some
Other Stuff

BONUS ONE:

As a purchaser of this book, I'd like to give you some bonuses. These include:

- information on how to become aware of your spirit guides
- information on how to connect with your spirit guides
- meditation for those who don't typically meditate and those who want a simple quick method of creating body harmony

You need only connect here to immediately receive these:
admin@YourLovingSpirit.com

BONUS TWO:

For anyone who takes the time to write a book review, please email **admin@YourLovingSpirit.com** with the name under which you left your review. I'll send you your personal Angel Codes to use. There's no obligation to leave a positive review. Naturally, I hope you enjoyed the book, but if you didn't, please let me know directly through **admin@YourLovingSpirit.com**

Need to reach me?

See my website at

www.YourLovingSpirit.com

or contact me through

admin@YourLovingSpirit.com

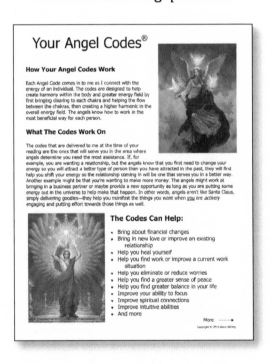

FOOTNOTES

* Names with asterisks have been changed; all other names are real and are given with the permission of those individuals.

1 **From Wikipedia:** The caduceus is the staff carried by Hermes in Greek mythology. The same staff was also borne by heralds in general, for example by Iris, the messenger of Hera. It is a short staff entwined by two serpents, sometimes surmounted by wings. In Roman iconography it was often depicted being carried in the left hand of Mercury, the messenger of the gods.

As a symbolic object it represents Hermes (or the Roman Mercury), and by extension trades, occupations or undertakings associated with the god. In later Antiquity the caduceus provided the basis for the astrological symbol representing the planet Mercury. Thus, through its use in astrology and alchemy, it has come to denote the elemental metal of the same name.

By extension of its association with Mercury and Hermes, the caduceus is also a recognized symbol of commerce and negotiation, two realms in which balanced exchange and reciprocity are recognized as ideals. This association is ancient, and consistent from the Classical period to modern times. The caduceus is also used as a symbol representing printing, again by extension of the attributes of Mercury (in this case associated with writing and eloquence).

Due to historical confusion between the caduceus and the traditional medical symbol, the rod of Asclepius, the caduceus is mistakenly used as a symbol of medicine and medical practice, especially in North America. The Rod of Asclepius has only a single snake and no wings, so is similar in form to the caduceus with its two snakes and often with wings.

2 **From Wikipedia:** Bone reabsorption is the process by which osteoclasts break down bone and release the minerals resulting in a transfer of calcium from bone fluid to the blood.

ABOUT THE AUTHOR

L INDA lives on a small property that overlooks the Columbia River in western Washington State.

Linda is an internationally best-selling author, writing coach, speaker, and spiritual healer. She works with people across the globe to help them acknowledge and embrace their own abilities to heal; to discover their innate soul-strength and all that encompasses; and she teaches them how to live purposely and without fear.

The world is full of magic things,
patiently waiting for our senses to grow sharper.

W.B. YEATS